THE ULTIMATE GUIDE TO FINANCIAL LITERACY FOR KIDS

MASTER MONEY SKILLS WITH FUN AND
INTERACTIVE WAYS TO SAVE, BUDGET, SPEND
WISELY, AND INVEST WITH CONFIDENCE

MONEY MENTOR PUBLICATIONS

CONTENTS

INTRODUCTION

All right, friends, gather around! Let me tell you a story about Alex. Alex had been saving up allowances and birthday money for what felt like forever, eyeing this super cool, almost magical remote-controlled drone. But then, out of the blue, a shiny new video game caught Alex's eye, threatening to derail all those months of saving. The struggle was real: to save or to spend, that was the question. Sound familiar? Yep, we've all been there, stuck in a real financial conundrum.

This is where I come in. I'm incredibly excited to teach you all the ins and outs of handling money. Why, you ask? Because coming to grips with your green (money, not vegetables!) from a young age is like having a superpower. My mission, should you choose to accept it, is to make the maze of money matters not just simple but super fun to navigate.

This book isn't your average, dry-as-toast guide to financial literacy. Nope, it's your golden ticket to becoming a money mastermind. Through relatable scenarios and brain-tickling activities at the end of each chapter, we'll embark on an epic adventure. We'll cover it all, from the basics of budgeting, the secrets of saving, and the ins and outs of investing to the wonders of wise spending. And the best part? It's going to be a blast!

Now, before we dive headfirst into this financial fiesta, let me share a little secret with you. Once upon a time, I, too, was baffled by dollars and cents. It took a handful of mistakes and a bucket load of lessons to get where I am today, financially independent and able to buy the things I need and want. So believe me when I say I get it. And that's exactly why I'm here, ready to guide you through the twists and turns of money management.

As we journey together through the pages of this book, I encourage you to jump into the activities, ponder the discussions, and have an ah-ha moment or two. What do you say? Ready to crack the code on cash, conquer your financial fears, and have a little fun along the way? Let's do this!

CHAPTER 1
MONEY MATTERS

Have you ever considered that every time you reach for your piggy bank or wallet, you're not simply grabbing cash but holding a key to the world? Yep, you heard that right. Money isn't just paper and metal. It's a ticket to adventure, a bridge to dreams, and sometimes, a bit of a puzzle. This chapter, my friends, is where we crack the code on why money makes the world go 'round and why understanding its powers can turn you into a wizard in your own right.

1.1 WHY MONEY MATTERS: UNDERSTANDING ITS ROLE

Let's kick things off with a simple question: What is money? At first glance, it might seem like just pieces of paper or some coins that jingle in your pocket. But, oh, it's so much more. Money is a really powerful tool that humans invented to solve some pretty big headaches. Imagine trying to trade your skateboard for a new video game. How would you decide if it's a fair trade? And what if the person with the video game didn't want a skateboard? Enter money, the superhero solution to these dilemmas.

Medium of Exchange

The first superpower of money is its role as a medium of exchange. This means it can be traded for goods and services. Without money, we'd be stuck in a barter system. This means that we would need to trade something we have to get something in return. Picture trying to buy a candy bar by trading socks. Sounds tricky, right? Money simplifies this process. It's universally accepted, so you don't have to find someone who wants your specific item for trade. Instead, you hand over some cash, and voilà, that candy bar is yours. This system works because everyone agrees that money has value, making buying and selling as easy as pie.

Future Value

Next up is money's role as a storehouse of value. This means you can save it now and spend it later, and it will still hold its worth. Imagine burying a treasure chest of toys. Over time, those toys might get damaged or lose their appeal. Money, on the other hand, maintains its value over time, allowing you to plan for the future. Whether you're saving up for a new bike or stashing away birthday money for something bigger, money's ability to preserve value over time makes it possible to reach bigger goals.

Unit of Account

Money also acts as a unit of account. This is a fancy way of saying it helps us measure the value of different things in a consistent way. For instance, how do you decide if a video game is worth more than a movie ticket? Money allows us to compare the two by assigning a price to each. It's like having a universal measuring stick for value, making it easier for everyone to understand how much things are worth. This not only makes shopping easier but also helps businesses set prices and keep track of their finances.

Standard of Deferred Payment

Lastly, money serves as a standard of deferred payment. That sounds complex, but it's just a way of saying that money allows you to buy things now and pay for them later. Ever heard of a credit card? It's a tool that lets you do exactly that. You can purchase something today, and instead of paying with cash on the spot, you agree to pay the bank back in the future. This concept is crucial for big purchases, like a house or a car, where paying all at once might not be possible. It's all about trust; the seller trusts that money will hold its value over time, and you get the flexibility to manage your finances over a longer period.

So there you have it. Money isn't just pieces of paper and metal. It's a key player in our daily lives, making transactions smoother, letting us save for the future, keeping track of value, and allowing for future payments. Its roles are crucial not just in personal finance but also in the global economy. Understanding these roles gives you a solid foundation to build your financial literacy, turning you into a savvy saver, a wise spender, and an all-around money maestro.

1.2 EARNING YOUR FIRST DOUGH: HOW KIDS CAN MAKE MONEY

Gathering your own stack of cash isn't just for grown-ups with jobs. Nope, even as a kid, there are plenty of ways to get a taste of earning your own money and start filling up that piggy bank. Let's check out some cool ideas that can help you start earning and learning about the value of a dollar (or whatever currency you're into).

Allowances

First up, let's talk allowances. This is like your first dip into the world of earning. Some parents offer their kids allowances in exchange for doing chores around the house. Chores could be anything from making your bed or taking out the trash to helping with dishes. This setup is a great way to learn about responsibility and the sweet rewards that come after hard work. Plus, managing your allowance teaches you to make decisions about spending and saving. Think of it as your budget to manage every week or month.

Saving Birthday and Holiday Money

Birthdays and holidays can sometimes feel like hitting a jackpot, right? Gifts and money from family and friends start rolling in and spending it all in one go is tempting. Here's a thought: What if you saved a portion of that money instead? This is a fantastic way to boost your savings quickly. It also teaches you the value of delayed gratification—saving now for something bigger and better down the line. Maybe there's a new game, a gadget, or even a trip you've been dreaming about. Saving your gift money gets you closer to those goals, and it's an excellent practice for managing unexpected cash influxes.

Small Businesses for Kids

If you're feeling more entrepreneurial, starting a simple business could be your ticket to earning more dough. The classic lemonade stand is a great example, but don't stop there. Got a green thumb? How about offering to plant flowers or do some gardening for neighbors? Or if you're handy with a lawnmower, lawn mowing services could be in demand, especially during the summer. Neighbors don't enjoy cleaning up after their pets? Start a pooper scooper or a dog walking service. These small ventures can teach you heaps about running a business, from setting prices to marketing your services and handling your earnings. Remember, every big entrepreneur started small, and your lemonade stand or gardening service could be the beginning of something huge.

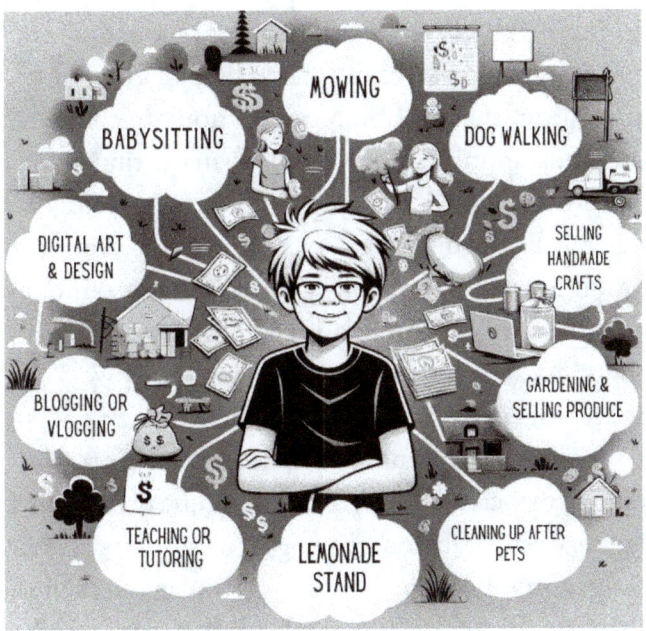

Turning Hobbies Into Income

Your hobbies are like seeds: They can grow into something more with a bit of care and creativity. Whether making jewelry, coding games, or baking cupcakes, there's a world out there eager to see what you can do. Here are a few pathways to consider:

- **Selling homemade crafts**: Kids who enjoy crafting can sell their creations, such as jewelry, keychains, or decorated notebooks, online through platforms like Etsy or eBay, at local craft fairs, or to friends and family.
- **Teaching or tutoring**: Older kids who excel in a subject or hobby, like a musical instrument, art, or coding, can offer lessons to younger kids in their community or online. And for the tech-savvy, how about teaching others how to use their gadgets or offering to set up new devices?
- **Blogging or vlogging**: Kids who are passionate about writing or making videos can start a blog or YouTube channel about their hobby. Monetization can come through ads, sponsorships, or affiliate marketing.
- **Performing arts**: Kids talented in singing, dancing, acting, or playing an instrument can perform at local events, community centers, or family gatherings to earn money.
- **Gardening and selling produce**: If gardening is their hobby, kids can sell the fruits, vegetables, or flowers they grow at local farmers' markets or directly to neighbors.
- **Digital art and design**: Kids skilled in digital art or graphic design can sell their artwork online or offer their design services for invitations, logos, or custom artwork.
- **Photography**: Budding photographers can sell their photos online through stock photography websites or offer their services for family portraits or local events.
- **Game streaming**: For kids who love video games, streaming on platforms like Twitch can eventually generate income through subscriber donations, ads, and sponsorships.

Tips for Parents

Offer guidance and support. Help your kids set up their ventures while teaching them about safety, especially online.

Marketing Your Hobby

Getting the word out there is like casting a spell; it only works if you have the right ingredients. Your passion is contagious, and with a dash of marketing, you can reach people who are just as excited about your hobby as you are. Consider these tips:

- With your parents' permission and help, use social media to showcase your work. Regular posts, engaging stories, and behind-the-scenes glimpses can attract a loyal following.
- Word of mouth is powerful. Encourage friends and family to spread the word about your products or services.
- Attend local fairs, markets, or community events where you can display your crafts, perform, or give a quick class. It's a great way to get noticed.

Earning your own money as a kid is a crash course in responsibility, hard work, and creativity. Whether through allowances, starting your own business, saving gift money, or finding unique ways to earn, each experience is packed with valuable lessons. Plus, watching your savings grow from your own efforts? That's a feeling of accomplishment money can't buy.

Success Stories

Inspiration surrounds us, with many young entrepreneurs turning their hobbies into success stories. Take, for instance, a teenager who started making candles in her kitchen and now runs a thriving online store, or a group of friends who turned their love for gaming into a popular YouTube channel that entertains and educates about coding and game design. Then there's the young artist who began sharing her drawings on social media and now sells prints and commissions worldwide.

Each story is unique, but they all share a common thread—a passion turned into a purpose, driven by creativity, hard work, and smart financial moves. These stories aren't just tales of success; they prove that with the right approach, your hobby can open doors to exciting opportunities.

Turning your hobby into a money-making venture is a mix of fun, work, and learning. It teaches you about doing what you love and sharing that love with the world while being smart about managing the financial side of things. It's a path that requires creativity, courage, and a bit of business savvy, and it's incredibly rewarding, offering lessons and experiences that go far beyond just making money. So go ahead, take that hobby of yours and see where it can lead you. Who knows? It may be the beginning of an amazing adventure.

1.3 THE CONCEPT OF EXCHANGE: MONEY FOR GOODS AND SERVICES

Imagine walking into your favorite candy store, eyes wide as you scan rows upon rows of sugary delights. You pick a chocolate bar and hand over a dollar; the treat is yours. This simple act is a classic example of an exchange. Money doesn't just sit pretty in your wallet. It's the key that unlocks the vast world of goods and services.

Basics of Buying and Selling

At its heart, buying and selling are about exchange. You offer money, and in return, you get something you want or need: a chocolate bar, a new scooter, or a haircut. This exchange is fundamental to how markets work. Businesses provide goods or services, and people like you and me use money to buy them. It's a dance that's been going on for centuries, shaping economies big and small.

What makes this dance interesting is the decision-making process. Every time you decide to buy something, you're answering basic questions. Is this chocolate bar worth my dollar? Could my money be better spent elsewhere? These decisions are influenced by several factors, including how much you value what you're buying and how much money you have to spend.

The Role of Prices

Prices are like signals in the market. They communicate the value of goods and services, guiding both buyers and sellers. But have you ever wondered how prices are set? It might seem like magic, but there's a method to the madness.

Prices often start with costs. For a product to be sold, it must first be made, which costs money. Materials, labor, even the electricity to run machines—all these costs add up, and they influence the final price of a product. But costs aren't the only factor. Remember how we talked about decisions? How much people are willing to pay for something also plays a big role in setting prices. If everyone's clamoring for the latest video game, the price might be higher because the perceived value is high.

Supply and Demand

Now, let's get into the nitty-gritty of supply and demand, two forces that drive the market like no other. Supply is how much of something is available. Demand is how much people want it. These two have a love-hate relationship. When supply is high and demand is low, prices tend to drop. Why? Because sellers want to encourage more people to buy their surplus goods. Remember when fidget spinners first came out? Everyone wanted one (high demand) so prices were high. After a while, people lost interest and stopped buying them (low demand). But there were still a lot of them on store shelves, so the price dropped to encourage people to buy them.

On the flip side, prices can skyrocket when supply is low and demand is high. Think about concert tickets to see the biggest band in the world. There are only so many seats available and everyone wants in, so tickets cost a lot.

Understanding supply and demand can make you a smarter shopper. If you notice a new product flying off the shelves and prices rising, you might decide to wait until the hype dies down and supply catches up with demand. That way, you might get a better deal.

Making Informed Choices

Making informed choices about spending your money is like being a detective. You're gathering clues, weighing evidence, and making decisions that impact your happiness and wallet. Here's how you can sharpen your detective skills:

- **Needs vs. wants**: First, determine if what you're buying is a need (essential for living) or a want (nice to have). Needs come first, but it's okay to satisfy wants if you have the budget.

- **Value for money**: Think about the value your buying brings to your life. Is it something you'll use or enjoy often? Or will it end up forgotten in a drawer somewhere? Getting good value for your money means spending money on things that add meaning to your life.
- **Comparison shopping**: Don't just buy the first thing you see. Look around, compare prices, and check out reviews. You might find the same thing for cheaper somewhere else or discover that another product offers better quality for a similar price.
- **Long-term satisfaction**: Sometimes, spending a bit more upfront can save you money in the long run. Cheap stuff might break or wear out quickly while spending a bit more could get you something that lasts longer. It's all about looking at your purchases in terms of long-term satisfaction and savings.

Whenever you exchange money for goods or services, you make decisions that affect your financial future. By understanding the basics of buying and selling, the role of prices, and the dance of supply and demand, you equip yourself with the knowledge to make informed choices. Whether it's deciding when to buy, what to spend your money on, or how to get the most bang for your buck, being a savvy consumer puts you in the driver's seat of your financial journey.

Chapter 1 Review Activity

Across
2. Swapping one thing for another.
4. The importance, worth, or usefulness of something.
5. Money you keep, usually in a bank, to use later.
7. Using your money to try to make more money by buying things that could grow in value.
9. Borrowing money to buy something now and paying for it later.
12. The money you make when you sell something for more than it cost you.
13. Telling people about products or services to try to sell them.
14. How much of something is available to buy.

Down
1. Trading things you have for things you want without using money.
2. Someone who starts their own business.
3. The type of money used in a country.
6. The wealth and resources of a country or region, especially in terms of the making and selling goods and servies
8. Planning how to spend your money.
10. Extra money you pay when you borrow money or extra money you get when you save money.
11. Money given regularly, usually by parents to children.

Answer Key on Page 162

CHAPTER 2
UNLOCKING THE TREASURE CHEST: YOUR GUIDE TO SAVING WISELY

Picture this: You're on a quest, not for hidden treasure or mystic artifacts, but for something far more valuable, the secret to saving smart. In every epic tale, heroes need a trusty sidekick. In the world of finance, that sidekick is your savings strategy. It protects you against unexpected expenses, powers up your purchasing ability, and sets the stage for achieving those big, dreamy goals. So grab your financial compass, and let's navigate the seas of savings together.

2.1 PIGGY BANKS AND BEYOND: FUN WAYS TO SAVE

The journey to saving starts with finding the perfect vessel for your treasure. Think of your piggy bank not just as a container but as a companion on your financial adventure. There are all sorts of piggy banks out there. Some count your coins as you drop them in, others come in the shape of your favorite cartoon characters, and then there are digital piggy banks that connect to apps, tracking your savings with every deposit.

Selecting a piggy bank that makes you excited to save is crucial. If you're tech-savvy, a digital piggy bank might be your calling. Love something tactile? A classic ceramic piggy bank you can personalize with paint or stickers could be the way to go. Remember, the right piggy bank doesn't just hold your money, it reflects your personality and motivates you to keep adding to your stash.

Setting Savings Goals

Goals are the map that guides your saving quest. Without them, it's easy to wander off the path or lose sight of why you're saving in the first place. Start simple. You may be eyeing a new video game, planning a day out with friends, or saving for a shiny new electric scooter. Here's the trick: Write your goal on a sticky note and attach it to your piggy bank. Seeing your goal every day acts as a constant reminder and inspiration.

Tracking Progress

Visual aids are fantastic for tracking your savings progress. Create a chart or a progress bar and fill it in as your savings grow. It's like watching the loading screen on your favorite game, but this time, you're watching your financial goals come to life. Place your tracker next to your piggy bank or on your bedroom wall where you'll see it every day. Witnessing your progress can give you a real sense of accomplishment and push you to keep going.

Beyond the Piggy Bank

Once you've mastered the art of the piggy bank, it might be time to level up. Consider opening a savings account designed for kids or teens. Many banks offer accounts with no fees, teaching you the ropes of banking without the risk. With a savings account, your money isn't just sitting there. It's growing thanks to something called interest. Plus, having a bank account can make you feel like a bona fide adult, taking charge of your financial future.

Opening an account can be a family affair. Talk to your parents about helping you set one up. They can guide you through the process, from choosing the right bank to understanding how to make deposits. This step boosts your savings and teaches valuable lessons about how banks work and the importance of financial security.

Saving money is more than just hoarding coins. It's setting goals, tracking progress, and taking those first steps into the wider world of finance. Whether you're stuffing a piggy bank to its brim or managing your first bank account, every penny saved is a building block toward your financial independence. So keep feeding that piggy bank, chart your savings journey with pride, and remember, every saver starts small. Your future self will thank you for the treasures you're tucking away today.

2.2 SETTING SAVINGS GOALS: DREAMS ACHIEVED STEP BY STEP

So, you've got a piggy bank that's starting to feel like a family member, and you're ready to tackle some serious savings goals. It's like setting out on a quest to slay the dragon, except your dragon is that awesome thing you've been dreaming about. But how do you differentiate between a fleeting fancy and a genuine treasure worth pursuing? Let's dive in.

Identifying Wants and Needs

It's Saturday afternoon, and you're faced with a decision: Indulge in a giant tub of your favorite ice cream or stash away some cash for that new dirt bike. Here lies the battle between wants and needs. Wants are those sparkly, eye-catching things you can live without (yes, even that ice cream). Needs, on the other hand, are your essentials. Think of them as your quest's armor and weapons—necessary for survival.

To sort your wants from your needs, ask yourself: Will buying this help me in the long run? Or is it just for a quick happiness boost? A new bike could mean adventures with friends and a healthy hobby, while the ice cream... well, that's a fleeting pleasure. The trick is to balance between saving for needs and sprinkling in a few wants to keep the journey exciting.

When you're a kid, you might not want a lot of things. Maybe just some toys, books, and your favorite snacks. But as you get older, you'll start wanting more stuff, like cool gadgets, games, and saving for a car or college. The trick to being ready for all these wants is to start saving money now, while you don't need to spend much. Think of it like a video game, where you're collecting coins or points early on so you have plenty when the game gets tougher. Saving early gives you a big boost, like a superhero's head start, so you can handle bigger needs and wants as you grow up.

Breaking Down Goals

Why limit your dreams to the back yard when you can aim for the stars? Financial goals should be more than saving enough for a new game or a pair of sneakers. Think bigger—a college fund, your first car, or even starting your own business. These grand dreams push you to learn, grow, and think creatively about money.

SMART Goals

Setting a goal is one thing, achieving it is another. That's where SMART goals come into play. This method breaks down lofty ambitions into manageable steps:

- **Specific**: Clearly define what you want to achieve.
- **Measurable**: Set markers to track your progress.
- **Achievable**: Be realistic. It's good to stretch your abilities but stay within the realm of possibility.
- **Relevant**: Make sure the goal matters to you. There's no point working toward something you're not passionate about.
- **Time-bound**: Set a deadline. A goal without a timeline is just a wish.

For example, instead of saying, "I just want to save money," a SMART goal would be, "I will save $300 for a new bike by saving $25 from my allowance each month for the next 12 months."

Visualizing Success

Have you ever heard of athletes visualizing their wins? It works for financial goals, too. Creating a vision board can bring your goals to life. Grab a poster board or use a digital app and start collecting images that represent your financial aspirations. Place it somewhere you'll see daily. This constant visual reminder keeps your goals front and center, fueling your motivation to make them a reality.

Involving Family and Friends

Sharing your goals can turn them into a group effort. Your family could offer to match what you save dollar for dollar, or a friend will jump on board with a similar goal, turning it into a friendly competition. Talking about your goals makes it easier to stick to them and get help, and helps you feel less alone and more likely to succeed.

Setting ambitious goals is the first step in a larger adventure. It's about aiming high, crafting a plan, and taking consistent action toward making those dreams a reality. With SMART goals, visualization techniques, and the support of your crew, you're not just dreaming big, you're setting the sails for a successful financial journey.

Making Saving a Game

Who said saving money can't be a blast? Introducing gamification to your savings strategy can transform it from a chore into a challenge you're eager to beat. Set up a savings challenge with your friends or family—see who can save the most money in a month by cutting back on non-essentials. Or create a personal savings bingo card with squares for different saving tasks: "No Spend Day," "Do an Extra

Chore," "Save All Money Earned." Celebrate victories with non-monetary rewards, like an at-home movie night.

Leveraging Technology

In today's digital age, your smartphone (or your parent's phone) is your magic wand for savings. Financial apps can track your spending, round up purchases to save the difference, and even invest spare change. But let's not stop there. Use technology to compare prices in real time with barcode scanning apps, ensuring you always get the best deal. And for the wizards in training, setting up alerts for price drops on wanted items can mean big savings with minimal effort.

- With your parent's help, download budgeting apps to keep your spending in check.
- Use price comparison apps when shopping to always ensure the best deal.
- Set up price drop alerts for items on your wishlist.

DIY and Upcycling

The old becomes new with a flick of your wrist, or rather, with a bit of creativity and elbow grease. Before you throw something out or rush to buy new, ask yourself if it can be repurposed or fixed. Jars can turn into stylish organizers, old game pieces can be used to create a brand-new game. The internet is a treasure trove of do-it-yourself tutorials for just about anything. Not only does reusing save money, but it also reduces waste—a double win.

- Turn scrap fabric into bags, pillow covers, or even art supplies.
- Turn old bottles into vases or create wall art from magazine cutouts.

- Fix, rather than replace. Often, a simple YouTube tutorial is all you need to repair something.

Adjusting as You Grow

Your goals are living, breathing aspirations that evolve as you do. The financial target you set at the beginning of the year might not make sense six months down the line, and that's okay. Regularly looking at your goals allows you to tweak them, ensuring they still align with what's important to you. It's like updating a game; as you level up, your objectives might change, requiring new strategies and tools.

2.3 CELEBRATING MILESTONES: REWARDS ALONG THE WAY

Imagine reaching the top of a mountain after a long hike. You're out of breath, your legs are tired, but the view and the sense of accomplishment are unmatched. We aim for this feeling as we navigate our financial goals. Every milestone reached is like a checkpoint in our adventure, deserving its own moment of recognition and celebration. Here's how we can make these moments count and keep our spirits high without losing sight of the bigger picture.

Designing Rewards

Crafting a reward system is like planting little treasures along your path, encouraging you to keep moving forward. Plan a reward for every financial milestone that matches the effort it took to get there. If you've saved half of your target for that iPad you've been eyeing, why not treat yourself to a day out at your favorite park? The trick is to ensure these rewards stay within your savings plan. They should be thoughtful yet modest—reminders of your progress that spur you on rather than set you back. List your milestones for a particular goal.

Next to each, jot down a reward that feels appropriate. This list is your roadmap. It keeps you aware of the next celebration and motivates you to reach your goal.

Milestone Celebration Ideas:

- **Homemade trophy for "Saver of the Month"**: Craft a unique trophy using recycled materials to celebrate the family member who saved the most that month.
- **Special Family Game Night**: Use a small part of the savings to buy a new board game for the family to enjoy together, celebrating your financial achievement.
- **DIY Certificate of Achievement**: Create personalized certificates for each family member when they hit their savings goal, complete with fun titles and decorations.
- **Savings Goal Chart Party**: When the family savings chart is filled, have a party with homemade snacks or a movie

night at home.

- **Picnic in the park**: Pack a picnic with everyone's favorite homemade treats and head to the park to celebrate reaching a savings milestone.
- **Craft a savings scrapbook**: Start a scrapbook documenting your financial journey, adding photos, notes, and milestones achieved along the way.
- **Financial freedom jar**: Each time someone reaches a goal, they get to add a colorful marble or stone to a communal jar, visually showcasing your collective achievements.
- **Savings jars decorating contest**: Have a contest to decorate individual savings jars using a variety of craft supplies, and celebrate with a small prize for the most creative jar.
- **Write a family newsletter**: Include updates on your financial goals, achievements, and fun facts or jokes. Share it with family and friends to celebrate your progress.
- **Host a "Future Dreams" dinner**: Prepare a special meal at home where each family member shares their dreams for the future, funded by your ongoing savings.
- **Build a goal tracker wall**: Designate a wall or board in the house to track savings goals with colorful post-its or magnets. Celebrate when you need to add a new goal because the previous one was achieved.
- **Create a savings song or chant**: Collaborate on a fun song or chant about saving money and perform it together when you reach a milestone.
- **Plant a garden**: Dedicate a new plant or flower to each financial milestone achieved, creating a thriving garden of your accomplishments.
- **Memory box for receipts and notes**: Start a memory box where you keep receipts or notes related to your financial goals, adding a new item each time a goal is reached.

- **Financial goals vision board party**: When major milestones are hit, host a vision board party where each person creates a board depicting their future goals, fueled by financial success.

Balancing Rewards and Savings

The art of rewarding yourself while continuing to save is a delicate balance. You must find joy in the now while keeping your future goals in focus. One approach is to set aside a small percentage of what you save for your reward fund. For example, for every $100 saved, $5 goes into a separate "reward pot." This method keeps your primary savings intact while giving you something to look forward to. It's a win-win that celebrates your dedication without compromising your end goal.

Set Clear Boundaries

Decide on the percentage of your savings that will go toward rewards. Stick to this rule to keep things consistent and fair to both your present and your future self.

Non-Monetary Rewards

Rewards don't have to cost money. In fact, some of the most meaningful celebrations involve experiences or privileges rather than material goods. For small wins, you might get an extra hour of screen time on the weekend or you get to choose the family movie night film. Larger achievements could be marked by a day dedicated to your favorite activities, all chosen by you. These kinds of rewards enrich your life with experiences, not things, and they remind you that the journey toward your financial goals can be fun and fulfilling.

Creativity Is Key

Think outside the box for ways to celebrate that don't involve spending. There may be a skill you've wanted to learn, and now's the perfect time to start. Use your milestones as opportunities to enrich your life in diverse ways.

Reflecting on Achievements

Taking the time to reflect on what you've accomplished is crucial. You're not just patting yourself on the back, you're witnessing how each milestone brings you closer to your larger goals. Set aside some time after reaching a milestone to write down how you achieved it, what challenges you faced, and how you overcame those challenges. This reflection turns your achievements into learning experiences, giving you insights and strategies to apply to future goals. It transforms each milestone from a mere checkpoint into a stepping stone, paving your way to success.

Keep a Journal

Dedicate a section of your financial journal to reflections. After each milestone, fill in a new entry. Over time, this section will become a testament to your growth and a guidebook filled with personal wisdom.

2.4 THE POWER OF PATIENCE: WAITING FOR WHAT YOU WANT

Now, let's talk about the golden virtue of saving: patience. It's not just waiting; it's believing in the magic of tomorrow. Consider the story of Mia. Mia saved her allowance for a whole year to buy a professional-grade telescope. There were times when dazzling video games and trendy clothes tempted her, but Mia kept her eyes on the stars—literally. When she finally gazed through her new telescope, the stars weren't just bright, they were her reward for patience.

Patience teaches us that some dreams are worth the wait. It turns saving into an adventure rather than a chore. Every time you choose to save instead of spend, you're one step closer to your goal. It's not easy, especially when shiny temptations pop up, but remember Mia and her stars. Your telescope moment is just around the corner.

Delayed Gratification

Delayed gratification is a fancy term for waiting for the good stuff. It means choosing to hold off on smaller, immediate rewards so you can earn bigger, more fulfilling rewards down the line. Think of it like this: You could spend your allowance on a bunch of small toys now, or you could save up for that mega Lego set you've been eyeing for months. Choosing the latter is a classic case of delayed gratification. Delayed gratification isn't just about saving money. It trains your brain to seek long-term happiness and satisfaction.

Success Stories

Let's talk about Sam. Sam had his eye on a top-of-the-line gaming console. It was a big goal, especially for a kid. Instead of splurging on smaller items, Sam decided to save every penny he could. Birthdays, holidays, even doing extra chores for neighbors—every bit of money went into his savings. It took over a year, but the day Sam walked into the store and bought his console with his own money was unforgettable. That console was more than just a gaming device; it was a trophy, a reminder of his patience and determination.

Then there's Lucy. Lucy dreamed of going to a summer camp known for its amazing outdoor adventures. The catch? It was pretty pricey. Lucy got creative. She started her own business selling handmade bracelets. It was slow going at first, but she kept at it, saving every sale's proceeds. When summer rolled around, Lucy had enough to cover camp fees. The experience was incredible, packed with memories and friendships that would last a lifetime.

Activities to Build Patience

Building patience, especially when saving money, can be fun. Here are a few activities to try:

- **The savings calendar**: Create a colorful calendar dedicated to your savings goal. Add a sticker or stamp for each week or month you add money to your savings. Watching your calendar fill up over time is satisfying and visually reminds you of your progress.
- **The patience jar**: Get two jars and fill one with marbles or beads, each representing a portion of your savings goal. Each time you add money to your savings, move a marble to the other jar. Watching the second jar fill up is surprisingly motivating and makes the concept of saving more tangible.
- **Goal visualization**: Spend some time drawing or crafting a representation of your goal. It could be a poster of that bike you're saving for or a camera you want. Place it where you'll see it every day. This visual reminder of what you're working toward can help keep your focus on the long-term prize.

Relating Patience to Saving

Patience and saving money are like two peas in a pod. They go hand in hand, each strengthening the other. When you save, you're practicing patience, waiting for something you want rather than going for instant gratification. And as you become more patient, saving becomes easier. You start to see the bigger picture, understanding that some things are worth the wait.

Saving with patience also teaches valuable life lessons beyond just financial smarts. It builds character, teaching resilience, determination, and the ability to set and achieve goals. These skills are like superpowers, equipping you to tackle financial challenges and any obstacle life throws your way.

So take a moment next time you find yourself itching to spend your savings on something small. Think about your bigger goal, the one that requires a bit of waiting and a bit of patience. Remember, the most rewarding treasures are often those we wait for, those we save for, step by step, day by day.

2.5 FROM PENNIES TO DOLLARS: WATCHING YOUR SAVINGS GROW

Imagine your savings as a tiny seed you've just planted in the ground. At first, it doesn't look like much, but give it time, water, and care, and one day it'll sprout into a flourishing tree. In the world of savings, "interest" is the water and care that helps your money-seed grow. Banks offer interest as a thank-you for keeping your money with them. It's like they're renting the money from you and paying you rent in return. And the best part? You don't have to do anything extra! Your money grows all on its own.

Interest Explained

When you save money in a bank, the bank uses your money to lend to others. In return, they add interest, a percentage of your savings, to your account. It's a win-win. You get extra money just for saving, and the bank gets to use your funds for its operations. Think of interest as a reward for being patient and savvy with your savings.

Compound Interest

Now, let's talk about a real game-changer: compound interest. It's interest on top of interest. Imagine you save $100, and your bank offers you 10% interest annually. After the first year, you have $110. In the second year, you earn interest not just on your original $100 but also on the $10 interest from the first year. By the end of the second year, you have $121. This cycle continues, and over time, your savings balloon not just from your deposits but from the accumulating interest. Compound interest is like a snowball rolling down a big hill, gathering more snow, and getting bigger with each turn.

Real-World Examples

Let's meet Jamie and Taylor, two friends passionate about saving. Jamie started saving $20 every month from age 10, while Taylor waited until turning 15 to start saving the same amount. They both chose savings accounts with an interest rate that capitalized on the magic of compounding. By the time they were 25, Taylor had a respectable sum of $3,461.70, but Jamie, who started earlier, had significantly more at $6,339.25—all thanks to the head start and the power of compound interest.

As we wrap up this chapter, remember that every penny you save today is a step toward a brighter, more secure tomorrow. Watching your savings grow from pennies to dollars, thanks to the wonders of interest and compound interest, proves that even the smallest amount set aside can transform into significant savings. Play the long game, where patience, consistency, and time are your best allies. As we move forward, we'll explore how to make smart moves with the money you've grown, ensuring it continues to work for you and paving the way for a future filled with possibilities.

Chapter 2 Review Activity

V	I	S	I	O	N	B	O	A	R	D	U	G	T	K	J
C	Z	S	Y	K	F	E	J	N	Q	Y	P	M	N	Z	G
H	O	T	G	K	D	N	S	X	A	C	C	O	U	N	T
A	W	M	C	M	O	S	B	X	D	J	Y	Y	G	U	L
L	I	Q	P	H	K	P	A	I	I	R	C	N	N	D	N
L	E	V	X	O	S	R	E	V	G	Q	L	D	B	N	S
E	B	D	D	P	U	A	E	I	I	Y	I	Y	P	L	S
N	O	L	M	I	I	N	M	W	T	N	N	Y	A	X	S
G	N	J	V	W	N	G	D	E	A	I	G	O	T	W	C
E	B	C	B	E	H	T	G	I	L	R	G	S	I	T	K
P	T	U	S	C	Q	D	E	Y	N	O	D	M	E	W	U
G	R	Z	A	O	U	Y	V	R	B	G	H	G	N	X	X
Q	R	U	O	B	C	A	P	K	E	A	U	W	C	A	N
X	Z	E	G	G	C	T	C	M	C	S	N	C	E	B	T
U	I	D	H	P	G	U	X	O	F	I	T	K	U	N	R
F	O	H	T	C	R	C	M	E	K	X	E	J	Z	K	A

PiggyBank	Interest	Compounding
Challenge	Upcycling	Savings
Budget	Digital	Account
Patience	Goals	Reward
Visionboard		

Answer Key on Page 162

CHAPTER 3
THE SMART SPENDER'S PLAYBOOK

I magine you're at a carnival. Lights flashing, music blaring, and every game booth promises a chance at the grand prize. But here's the catch: You've only got a limited number of tickets to spend. Where do you use them? On the flashy, high-stakes games that catch your eye first? Or do you strategize, choosing the games that offer the best chance of winning or that you'll enjoy the most? This carnival is a lot like life's financial decisions. Every choice costs something. Making smart choices means knowing the difference between what you need and what you want, then acting wisely.

3.1 NEEDS VS. WANTS: MAKING SMART CHOICES

Defining Needs and Wants

Let's break it down. Needs are the essentials, the nonnegotiables: food, shelter, clothing (the basics, not a designer wardrobe), and maybe your education costs. Wants, on the other hand, are all the extras. They're the sprinkle on your ice cream, the neon lights on your bike, or that video game that's just been released. The tricky part? Sometimes, what we think we need is actually a want in clever disguise. Recognizing the difference is step one to smart spending.

Prioritizing Spending

Once you've separated your needs from your wants, it's time to play financial Tetris. Your budget is the game board, and you've got to fit in your needs first. The space that's left—that's where your wants come in. If there's room, great! If not, it's time to reassess and maybe decide which wants can wait. This doesn't mean cutting out fun. It just lets you make sure you've got your bases covered before adding on the extras.

The Envelope System

Here's a tactile way to manage your spending: the envelope system. Grab some envelopes and label each with a category like Food, Savings, Fun Money, you get the gist. Every time you get some cash, divide it among the envelopes based on your priorities. It's a visual and physical way to see how much money you have and make you stop spending when an envelope's empty. No more guessing if you can afford that comic book or if you should save a bit more.

Real-Life Decision Making

Now imagine you're at the store with money in your pocket. You spot a cool gadget you've been eyeing, but you also remember you're saving up for a camp next summer. Here's where you pause and think. Ask yourself, "Do I need this right now? Can it wait? What's more important in the long run?" Sometimes taking a moment to consider your options leads to smarter decisions. And hey, if you decide to wait, that gadget might be on sale by the time you've saved enough for it and the camp.

Making smart choices with your money doesn't mean you never get what you want. It means making sure you've got what you need first, then using your spending power wisely on the wants that truly matter to you. You're putting yourself in control, not letting impulse decisions lead the way. With practice, you'll find your balance. You'll become a savvy saver and a smart spender.

3.2 THE ART OF BUDGETING: PLANNING YOUR SPENDING

Picture this: You've got your own economy running. Money comes in, money goes out, and you're the boss in charge of it all. Sounds cool, right? But even bosses need a plan to make sure they're heading in the right direction. That's where a budget comes in. It's not just a list or a chart. It's your game plan for winning at money management. Let's break it down into steps and skills that'll make you a budgeting pro before you even realize it.

What Is a Budget?

Think of a budget as your personal finance map. It shows you what you're earning, what you're spending, and where you can save. It's like having a financial snapshot that helps you make decisions about your cash flow. Why bother? Well, with a budget, you can see if you're spending too much on video games and not enough on saving for that cool skateboard. It helps you set your spending limits and shows you where your money's going every month.

Creating a Simple Budget

All right, ready to set up your own budget? Here's a simple way to start:

1. **Track your money**: Write down everything you spend money on, no matter how much, for one week (or one month). Those candies and online game credits add up.
2. **Income vs. expenses**: List your income sources (allowance, chore money, birthday money, etc.) and your expenses (things you spend money on). Use your one-week track as a guide for your monthly expenses.
3. **Set categories**: Divide your expenses into categories like Needs, Wants, and Savings. It'll help you see where your money's going.
4. **Allocate funds**: Decide how much money goes into each category. As a kid who doesn't pay for a lot of your needs yet, you could decide to put 50% in savings and spend 30% on wants and 20% on needs. As you grow older, these percentages will change. You'll also make adjustments based on what you learn from tracking your spending.
5. **Tools**: Use a simple spreadsheet, a budgeting app, or good old paper and pencil to keep it organized.

Sticking to a budget

Sticking to a budget might sound tough, but making it a habit is worth the effort. Here are some ways to stay on track:

- **Weekly check-ins**: Once a week, take a few minutes to review your budget. It'll help you catch any overspending early, before you get off track.

- **Fun money**: Always include a category for Fun Money. This is money you can spend however you like, guilt-free. Knowing you have this can make sticking to the other parts of your budget easier.
- **Visual reminders**: Put a chart or a picture of what you're saving for in a place where you'll see it every day. It'll remind you why sticking to your budget is worth it.
- **Accountability buddy**: Team up with a friend or family member and share your budgeting goals. Sticking to a plan is easier when you know someone's rooting for you.

Adjusting Your Budget

Your budget isn't set in stone. Life changes and your budget should, too. Here's when and how to tweak it:

- **Regular reviews**: At the end of each month, compare your planned budget with what you actually spent. Look for patterns. You may be consistently overspending in one area or allocating too much to another.
- **Life changes**: Got a bump in your allowance? Or maybe there's a new expense on the horizon? Adjust your budget to reflect these changes.
- **Goal shifts**: If your financial goals change (say, now you're saving for a computer instead of a hoverboard), update your budget to match your new priorities.
- **Trial and error**: Feel free to experiment with your budget. You may prefer saving a little more for wants and a little less for needs. Adjust, try it out, and see how it goes.

Creating and sticking to a budget is a dynamic process. Find what works for you and tweak it as you go. With each adjustment, you'll learn more about your spending habits and how to manage your money better. Remember, the goal isn't to restrict your spending but to empower you to make smart choices with your money. With a solid budget, you're not just planning your spending—you're planning for success.

3.3 WISE SHOPPER TACTICS: GETTING MORE BANG FOR YOUR BUCK

So, you've got your eyes on the prize—that epic gadget that's been calling your name. But wait! Before you hand over your hard-earned cash, let's put on our detective hats and dig into some tactics that ensure you're not just spending wisely but you're also getting the most bang for your buck.

Comparing Prices

In the internet age, finding the best deal is like a treasure hunt—exciting, rewarding, and sometimes challenging. Here's the scoop: Always check different stores (both online and in person) for the price of the item you want. Apps and websites can scan a broad range of retailers to show you where to find the best deal. Sometimes, the price difference can be eye-opening. It might mean waiting a bit longer for shipping or a trip to a different store, but the savings can be worth the extra effort. (See Chapter 10.3 for a list of helpful websites and apps.)

- Tip: Use price comparison tools or apps. They do the heavy lifting by comparing prices across multiple sites in real-time.
- Exercise: Next time you're shopping, pick an item and compare its price in at least three different places. Note the differences and where you find the best deal.

Understanding Value

Here's a little secret: The best deal isn't always the cheapest option. Shocking, right? But think about it—value is about more than just the price tag. It's about what you're getting for your money. A toy might be cheaper at one store, but if it's a lower-quality version that'll break in a week, is it really worth it? Assessing value means looking at durability, warranty, and how much use you'll get out of it. Sometimes, paying a bit more upfront for something that lasts longer or provides more enjoyment is the smarter move.

Reflection

Think of something you bought because it was cheap then later regretted buying it. Now, think of a purchase that was a bit more expensive, but you felt it was worth every penny. What made the difference?

Coupons and Sales

Coupons and sales are like the secret codes of shopping. They can unlock deals and discounts that make your money stretch further. Here's how you can become a coupon whiz:

- Keep an eye on sales cycles. Many stores have predictable patterns for marking down items or offering special sales. After the holidays is a common time for big discounts.
- With your parents' permission and help, sign up for newsletters and loyalty programs. Your inbox might get a bit fuller, but you'll be in the loop for exclusive coupons and sale alerts.
- Use coupon apps and websites. They compile current coupons and promo codes in one place, making it easy to

find discounts for the stores you love. Make sure your parents are okay with the site before you use it.

- Create a coupon organizer. It can be a simple folder or a digital document where you keep track of coupons, sale dates, and promo codes. Make a habit of checking it before making a purchase.

Quality vs. Quantity

There's an age-old debate: Is it better to have many things that might not last or a few really good items? Here's a thought—investing in quality means you buy less often because your stuff doesn't wear out as quickly. It's like choosing between a cheap pair of shoes that fall apart after a few months and a more expensive pair that lasts for years. In the long run, the pricier pair is actually the better deal. Plus, it's kinder to our planet. Less waste, less clutter, and more value for you.

Consider Alex's experience. He decided to buy a high-quality backpack instead of the cheaper option. While his friends were on their third or fourth backpacks two years later, Alex's was still going strong, looking as good as new. The initial price was higher, but the cost per use was much lower.

Navigating the world of smart shopping is more than just finding the lowest price. When you become a savvy spender, you know how to compare prices, assess the true value of a product, take advantage of sales and coupons, and choose quality over quantity. With these tactics in your toolkit, you're investing your money in a way that brings you the most joy, use, and satisfaction. Remember, every smart purchase is a step toward becoming a more empowered, informed, and wise consumer.

3.4 AVOIDING IMPULSE BUYS: THINK BEFORE YOU SPEND

Have you ever walked past a store where a shiny new gadget caught your eye, whispering sweet nothings like, "Buy me now!" into your brain? That, my friends, is the siren call of an impulse buy. It's that thing you didn't know you "needed" until you saw it, and now, suddenly, you can't imagine life without it. But here's the kicker: More often than not, these purchases end up forgotten, gathering dust, or worse, causing a twinge of regret. Let's navigate this tricky terrain with some smart strategies.

What are Impulse Buys?

Impulse purchases are like those sneaky snack attacks. They happen fast, driven by emotion rather than need or planning. One minute, you're fine, and the next, you're itching to spend on something that wasn't even on your radar. These buys can be problematic because they munch away at your budget, leaving less for what you're saving up for.

The 24-hour Rule

Here's a nifty trick to combat those impulsive urges: the 24-hour rule. It's simple. When you feel the pull toward an unplanned purchase, pause and give yourself a full day to think it over. This brief break allows the initial "gotta have it" rush to fade, giving you time to consider whether you really want or need the item. You'll often find that the urge diminishes or that the item wasn't as essential as it seemed just yesterday.

Set Spending Limits

Another way to keep impulse buys in check is by setting clear spending limits for different categories of purchases. This means deciding on a specific amount you're comfortable spending on things like entertainment, clothes, or eating out each month. Once you hit that limit, spending is a no-go zone until the next month rolls around. This boundary helps you stay mindful of your spending and keeps your budget on track.

- Break your budget down into categories.
- Assign a monthly spending limit to each category.
- Stick to these limits, and if a category runs dry, wait until you refill it before buying anything else.

Reflection and Regret

Ever bought something on a whim and then wondered, "Why did I even get this?" You're not alone. Reflecting on past impulse purchases can be a powerful way to learn and grow. Take time to think about purchases you regret, how they made you feel afterward, and what you could have done differently. Don't reflect just to beat yourself up. Learn from the past so you can make smarter choices in the future.

- Keep a small journal or list of purchases you regret and why you regret them.
- Review this list when you're tempted to make an impulse buy.

By understanding the nature of impulse buys, employing the 24-hour rule, setting firm spending limits, and reflecting on past regrets, you'll equip yourself with a robust toolkit to combat those spur-of-the-moment spending urges. You'll become more intentional with your money, ensuring each purchase adds real value to your life.

As we wrap up this exploration into smart spending tactics, remember that the power lies in your hands (or wallet). The strategies we've discussed are tools to help you make choices that align with your goals, values, and financial well-being. Heading into the next chapter, we'll pivot from saving and spending to the exciting world of making your money grow. Think of it as moving from defense to offense in the game of financial literacy. Ready to level up?

Chapter 3 Review Activity

Across
1.Things you must have to live and be safe, like food, a place to live, and clothes (but not the fancy kind).
2.All the extra fun stuff you like, such as toys, games, or treats, but don't really need to live.
5. Money set aside for future use or emergencies.
8. A cool trick where you wait a whole day before buying something you suddenly want, to see if you still really want it later.
9. Special tickets that let you buy stuff for less money, like getting a dollar off your favorite ice cream.
10. How good or sturdy something is. Sometimes spending more on something that lasts longer is smarter than buying the cheapest option.
12. When stores lower prices on items for a short time so you can get things you need or want for less money.

Down
3.It's like a plan for how to spend your allowance or birthday money so you can buy things you need, save some, and still have fun.
4.A method of dividing cash into categories for spending or saving.
5.Planning and tactics used to manage financial resources effectively.
6.Buying something suddenly without thinking it through, like grabbing a candy bar while waiting in line at the store.
7.The action of arranging or dealing with something according to its importance.
11. A small cool tool or device, often something new and fun, like a smartphone or a video console.

Answer Key on Page 162

CHAPTER 4
MAKING YOUR MONEY GROW: THE BEGINNER'S GUIDE TO INVESTING

Why do some people seem to have a magic touch when it comes to money? It's like they've got a green thumb, but instead of growing epic tomatoes, they're growing their cash. Here's the secret: It's not magic, it's investing. Think of investing as planting your money seeds in different pots and watching them sprout and bloom into a lush garden. Intrigued? Let's dig into the soil of investing and uncover how you can start growing your financial garden today.

4.1 WHAT IS INVESTING? MONEY MAKING MONEY

Investing is like leveling up in a video game. Instead of keeping your money under the mattress (or in a savings account where it slowly grows), you put it out into the world where it can work harder for you. When you invest, you buy things you believe will increase in value over time. These could be pieces of a company (stocks), loans you give out (bonds), or even a savings account that pays you interest.

The goal? To make your initial pile of money bigger without having to mow more lawns or babysit more kids.

Types of Investments

Let's break down your investment options:

- **Stocks**: Buying a stock means you own a tiny slice of a company. If the company does well, your slice becomes more valuable. Imagine owning a piece of your favorite video game company and getting a share of their profits!
- **Bonds**: These are like IOUs from the government or companies. You lend them money, and they promise to pay you back with a little extra added on. It's as if you're the bank, and they're taking a loan from you.
- **Savings accounts**: Not all investments require buying stocks or bonds. A high-yield savings account also counts. It's a cozy, low-risk spot for your money to grow bit by bit.

Risk vs. Reward

This is a crucial piece of the puzzle: the risk vs. reward balance. Investing can be a bit of a roller coaster. Stocks might offer big rewards, but they also come with the risk of losing value. Bonds are usually steadier, but they grow slower. It's like choosing between a wild, unpredictable game with high scores and the possibility of losing points, or a slower, more predictable one where you steadily accumulate points. The key is finding the right mixture that matches your comfort with risk and your dreams for the future.

The Long-Term Perspective

Investing is a marathon, not a sprint. You play the long game, letting your money grow over years, even decades. Think of a tree growing from a sapling to a giant oak. It doesn't happen overnight. That's how investing works. It takes patience and time, but the rewards can be worth it. You're not just saving for something a year from now. You're building wealth that can support your dreams far into the future.

Investing your money is an exciting step toward financial independence. By understanding the basics, like the different types of investments and the balance between risk and reward, you're laying down the foundation for a prosperous future. You're making your money work for you, growing your financial garden one investment at a time. So grab your financial tools, and let's start planting those money seeds.

4.2 SIMPLE INVESTMENT OPTIONS FOR KIDS

When you think about investing, you might picture people in suits furiously trading stocks on Wall Street. But guess what? Even as a kid, you have some cool options to start growing your own pot of gold. Let's peel back the curtain on some investment choices that are kid-friendly and great learning opportunities.

Savings Accounts With Interest

You know that piggy bank sitting on your shelf? Imagine if, every month, it magically had a little more money in it just because you'd been keeping your savings there. That's how a savings account with interest works. Banks reward you for letting them hold onto your money by paying you interest, a percentage of your savings. Here's why it's a solid first step into the world of investing:

- **Safety:** Your money is super safe in a bank. Even if the bank were to run into trouble, insurance covers your cash up to a certain amount.
- **Easy access**: Need to dip into your savings? No problem. You can get to your money easily, which is great for unexpected expenses or when you've finally saved enough for that big purchase.
- **Learning to save**: Watching your balance grow with interest can be a big motivator to save more. It's like getting paid just for being smart with your money.

Certificates of Deposit (CDs)

Think of CDs as a special ticket you buy for a money-growing ride. When you get a certificate of deposit, you tell the bank, "Hey, you can use my money for a bit." In return, they promise to pay you more interest than a regular savings account. The catch? You agree not to touch your money for a certain period, like six months or a year. Here are some reasons why CDs can be awesome:

- **Higher interest rates**: Because you agree to leave your money alone for a while, banks pay you more interest.
- **Time choices**: You can pick how long you want to lock in your money based on how long you think you can wait.
- **Safe and predictable**: CDs are a safe bet. You know exactly how much money you'll have at the end, no surprises.

Stock Market Basics

Owning a piece of a company might sound like big business, but it's actually something kids can do, too. When you buy stocks, you get a small part of a company. If the company does well, your piece of the pie could become more valuable. Here's the scoop:

- **Ownership**: Buying stock means you own a tiny fraction of that company. You're like a mini-business owner.
- **Potential for growth**: If the company grows, so does the value of your stock. Some people have made their money grow a lot by picking the right stocks.
- **Learning opportunity**: Following your stocks can teach you loads about businesses, how they make money, and what makes them grow.

Investment Apps for Beginners

In today's digital world, there are apps for just about everything, including investing. Some super-cool apps are designed just for beginners and even allow you to practice investing without using real money. This way, you can get a feel for how investing works without any risk. Why these apps rock:

- **Simulated investing**: Many apps offer a simulated investing experience, giving you play money to invest in real stocks and see how they do.
- **Educational tools**: These apps are packed with tutorials, articles, and quizzes to help you learn the ropes of investing.
- **Real-life practice**: By using a simulated environment, you can practice buying and selling stocks, all based on real market data, which is cool for getting your feet wet in the investing world.

Diving into investing might seem like jumping into the deep end, but with these kid-friendly options, you're actually wading into the shallows where it's safe to learn and grow your money. From the steady climb of interest in savings accounts and CDs to the exciting world of stocks and simulated investing apps, there's a whole landscape of opportunities out there. Who knew you could have this much fun watching your money grow?

4.3 RISKS AND REWARDS: THE INVESTMENT SCALE

Investing your allowance or birthday money is different from buying a new video game or skateboard. When you decide to invest, you're stepping onto a seesaw of risks and rewards. These seesaw tips are based on the choices you make, and understanding how to balance them is part of becoming a smart investor.

Understanding Volatility

First off, volatility is a big word that often pops up when talking about investing. Simply put, it means the price of your investment can jump up and down like a kangaroo on a trampoline. One day, your investment in a cool tech company might be up, making you feel like a millionaire, and the next day, it could drop, making your heart sink.

Why does this happen? Because lots of things affect investment prices, like how well the company is doing, changes in the economy, or even news stories. Imagine if a video game company announces a hot new game release. People get excited and want to buy more stock, and the price goes up. But if something goes wrong, say, a glitch in the game that delays the launch, the price might go down.

Diversification

To avoid putting too much stress on our seesaw with volatility, we use a strategy called diversification. This might sound complicated, but it's just a fancy way of saying, "Don't put all your eggs in one basket." If you only invest in one thing, like a single stock or bond, and it takes a nosedive, you could lose a lot. But if you spread your money out over different types of investments, you're less likely to feel a big hit if one doesn't do well.

Think of it like this: Instead of saving up for that one big, expensive video game, you also pick up a couple of smaller, cheaper games. If the big game turns out to be a dud, you're not as bummed because you've got other games to enjoy. It's the same with investing. Having a mix—some stocks, some bonds, maybe a bit in a savings account—can keep your money growing steadily, even if one investment doesn't perform as expected.

Researching Before Investing

Before diving into any investment, doing your homework is key. This means spending time looking into what you're thinking about putting your money into. It's a bit like when you're eyeing that next big game purchase. You read reviews, watch gameplay videos, and even check out what other gamers are saying online.

With investing, it's similar. You'd look at how the investment has done in the past, what experts are saying about its future, and any news that might affect its performance. It's important because the more you know, the better choices you'll make. Sure, it takes a bit more time, but it's worth it to help your money grow and avoid any surprise drops in your investment's value.

The Role of Patience

Lastly, let's talk about patience—again. If investing had a best friend, patience would be it. Making your money grow through investing won't be a quick path to becoming rich. You'll have to set your sights on the horizon and wait for your investments to mature over time.

Here's the thing: Markets go up and down. That's just what they do. But over the long term, they tend to go up more than they go down. That means if you're patient and stick with your investments, and don't panic when things look a little rocky, there's a good chance your money will grow.

So remember, investing is more like growing a tree than zapping a video game boss. Trees take time to grow tall and strong, and so does your investment. The trick is to water it (with regular contributions), protect it from pests (by not making hasty decisions when the market dips), and give it time to grow. You'll see your money garden flourish with patience, turning those initial seeds into a lush canopy of financial well-being.

In the end, balancing the seesaw of risks and rewards in investing is a skill that grows with you. The more you understand volatility, the importance of diversification, the power of research, and the value of patience, the more equipped you'll be to make your money work hard for you. And while investing comes with its ups and downs, embracing these concepts will help you navigate the path to financial growth with confidence and savvy.

4.4 FUTURE FINANCIAL HEROES: KID INVESTORS' STORIES

In a world where kids are making big waves, let's spotlight some young investors who've turned their pocket money into impressive portfolios. These tales are blueprints for budding financial geniuses everywhere. Each narrative brings to life the ups and downs of investing from a kid's perspective, offering invaluable insights and inspiration.

A Tale of Two Siblings: Ella and Max's Lemonade Stand Venture

Ella and Max, a dynamic sister-brother duo at ages 10 and 12, decided to invest their lemonade stand earnings in stocks. They chose companies they knew and loved, like the makers of their favorite video games and snacks. It wasn't all smooth sailing. One of their chosen companies faced a recall, causing their shares to dip. But they held on, learning early that the market has good and bad days. Over time, their patience paid off, teaching them the critical lesson of sticking through the rough patches for eventual gain.

- **Lesson learned**: Even when the market looks grim, perseverance can lead to sweet rewards.
- **Advice**: "Invest in what you know and love. It makes the ups and downs more relatable," says Ella.

From Piggy Bank to Portfolio: Sarah's Journey

At 8, Sarah was given a few shares of a tech giant as a gift. Intrigued by the idea of owning a piece of a big company, she started doing chores and saving birthday money to buy more shares. By 14, Sarah had diversified her portfolio to include renewable energy and health-care stocks. She faced challenges, like when one stock plummeted due to an unexpected scandal. However, Sarah's diversified approach meant her overall portfolio remained strong.

- **Lesson learned**: Diversification is like a safety net, keeping you steady when individual investments fall.
- **Advice**: "Don't put all your eggs in one basket. Spread them out," Sarah advises.

The Accidental Investor: Liam's Story

Liam stumbled into investing at age 9 when he mistakenly clicked on an app advertisement offering virtual stock trading. With his parents' guidance, he began exploring the world of simulated stock investments, using virtual money to buy and sell. This safe, risk-free environment was the perfect playground for Liam to learn the ins and outs of the stock market, teaching him valuable lessons about research, timing, and market trends without any real-world losses.

- **Lesson learned**: Starting with simulated investments can be a fantastic, risk-free way to learn.
- **Advice**: "Use virtual trading apps to practice. It's like a video game, but you learn to invest," Liam suggests.

Starting Small, Dreaming Big: The Collective Wisdom

These stories underline a powerful message: Beginning your investing journey doesn't require a fortune. With just a few dollars and a dash of curiosity, any kid can embark on the path to becoming an investor. The key is to start small, stay patient, and keep learning. Here's a roundup of advice from our young investors:

- **Understand what you're investing in**: Take the time to learn about the companies or products you want to invest in.
- **Patience pays off**: Don't expect overnight success. Investing is about playing the long game.

- **Embrace mistakes**: Every misstep is a learning opportunity. Reflect on what went wrong and how you can improve.
- **Keep it fun**: Choose investments in businesses or sectors you're genuinely interested in. It makes the process enjoyable and personal.
- **Seek advice**: Don't be shy about asking parents, teachers, or financial advisors for insights. A little guidance can go a long way.

By weaving together these threads of wisdom, it becomes clear that investing isn't just for adults with big bank accounts. It's a realm where curious kids, armed with a bit of know-how and a lot of determination, can thrive and grow their financial futures.

As we wrap up this chapter, remember that the world of investing is vast and varied, offering endless opportunities to those willing to explore. From the stories of Ella, Max, Sarah, and Liam, we gather not just inspiration but also practical strategies for embarking on our own investing adventures. Whether it's through direct stock purchases, simulated trading apps, or starting with a simple savings account, the journey to financial growth begins with a single step. As we look ahead, let's carry forward the lessons learned, the advice shared, and the undeniable truth that age is just a number in the world of investing. The next chapter awaits, promising new financial landscapes to navigate and conquer.

CHAPTER 5
THE CREDIT CHRONICLE: NAVIGATING THE WORLD OF BORROWING WISELY

I magine you're at your favorite arcade. You've played all the games you're good at, racking up points like a pro. Now, you're eyeing the grand prize in the display case, but your points fall short. Here's where credit comes into play at the arcade of life. Instead of points, you're dealing with real money. Credit can be that bridge to reach what you want sooner, whether it's a new bike, a college education, or your first car. But, just like any arcade game, there are rules to play by to win.

5.1 THE BASICS OF BORROWING: GOOD DEBT VS. BAD DEBT

Credit is essentially a trust system. It's a way to borrow money with the promise to pay it back later, often with interest. Think of it like a friend lending you money to buy a game today because you don't have enough cash on hand, and you agree to pay them back after your next allowance. In this case, the friend is a bank or credit institution, and they'll charge you for the service.

Good Debt vs. Bad Debt

Not all debts are created equal. Some can actually work in your favor.

- **Good debt**: This is the kind that can help you advance in life. For example, taking a loan for college is seen as good debt. It's an investment in your education, potentially leading to better job opportunities and income in the future. Another example could be a mortgage for a house, which typically increases in value over time.
- **Bad debt**: This type usually results from buying things that won't increase in value and that you can't afford. High-interest credit card debt from buying the latest gadgets or designer clothes falls into this category. These items don't earn you money over time and might even lose value the moment you purchase them.

The Cost of Credit

Borrowing money isn't free. The extra cost comes in the form of interest, which can add up quicker than you'd expect. The interest rate, often a percentage, is what lenders charge you for borrowing money. It's like paying rent on the money you borrow.

- For example, if you take out a $100 loan with a 10% annual interest rate, you'll owe $110 at the end of the year. If you don't pay a loan off quickly, interest can make the total amount you owe grow larger and larger.

Building a Positive Credit History

Starting early on, building a good credit history can open doors for you in the future. Here's how to set yourself up for credit success:

- **Always pay on time**: This is the golden rule. Late payments can hurt your credit score, making it harder and more expensive to borrow money in the future.
- **Start small**: A low-limit credit card or a small loan, paid off regularly, can help you begin to build a good credit history.
- **Stay below your limit**: Try not to max out your credit cards. Using a small portion of your available credit looks better on your credit report.
- **Monitor your credit**: Know your credit score and look at your credit report. This way, you can catch any mistakes and understand how your behavior with money affects your credit.

Debt Responsibility Quiz

Take this quiz to see how well you understand the concepts of good and bad debt, interest rates, and the basics of credit. Each question gives feedback and tips to improve your borrowing smarts.

1. What is debt?

 A. Money that you find on the street.
 B. Money that you earn from a job.
 C. Money that you borrow from someone else and need to
   pay back.
 D. Money that you keep in a piggy bank.

Answer: Debt is money that you borrow from someone else, like a bank or a friend, which you need to pay back later, often with extra money called interest. (Answer C)

Feedback & tips: Remember, borrowing should be done wisely. Always ask yourself if what you're borrowing for is necessary or if it can wait until you have enough money saved up.

2. Can debt be a good thing?

 A. No, because it's always bad to owe money.
 B. Yes, when you use it to buy all the video games you want.
 C. Yes, when it's used for something that benefits you in the
   long run.
 D. No, because you should never spend money.

Answer: Yes, debt can be good when it's used for something that will benefit you in the long run, like an education that helps you get a better job. (Answer C)

Feedback & tips: Think of good debt as an investment in your future. But be careful to only borrow what you need and can pay back comfortably.

3. What is bad debt?

A. Borrowing money to buy a house.
B. Money borrowed for things that lose value quickly.
C. Taking a loan for education.
D. Saving money in a bank.

Answer: Bad debt is money borrowed for things that lose value quickly or don't provide a return on your investment, like spending on toys or a fancy vacation. (Answer B)

Feedback & tips: Before making a purchase with borrowed money, consider if it's something you really need or if there's a cheaper alternative.

4. What are interest rates?

A. A fee you pay to use a shopping cart.
B. The extra percentage of borrowed money you pay to the lender.
C. The rate at which your pocket money increases.
D. A type of rate used in cooking recipes.

Answer: Interest rates are the percentage of the borrowed amount you have to pay extra to the lender for allowing you to use their money. (Answer B)

Feedback & tips: Always look for the lowest interest rate when borrowing money. You'll always have to pay more than you borrowed, but higher rates mean you'll have to pay even more extra.

5. How does credit work?

A. By only using cash for purchases.
B. It allows you to borrow money or buy things with a promise to pay back later.
C. It works like magic.
D. You get unlimited money.

Answer: Credit allows you to borrow money to buy things with a promise to pay the money back later. Good credit means you're trusted to pay back the money on time. (Answer B)

Feedback & tips: Always pay back borrowed money on time to build good credit. This shows lenders that you're responsible with money.

6. What happens if you don't pay back debt?

A. You may face extra fees, higher interest rates, and a lower credit score.
B. You get a reward.
C. Nothing happens.
D. You receive more money.

Answer: Not paying back debt can lead to extra fees, higher interest rates, and a lower credit score. This means it will be harder to borrow money in the future. (Answer A)

Feedback & tips: If you're having trouble paying back debt, talk to the lender right away to discuss your options. They may be able to help you with a payment plan.

7. Why is budgeting important when you have debt?

  A. Because it's a fun hobby.
  B. It helps you manage your spending to ensure you can pay
     back your debts.
  C. Budgeting is not important.
  D. It increases your debt.

Answer: Budgeting helps you keep track of your spending and make sure you have enough money to pay back your debts while still covering your other expenses. (Answer B)

Feedback & tips: Start a simple budget by listing your income and expenses. This will help you see where your money is going and find ways to save.

8. What is a savings account, and how can it help with debt?

  A. A type of game.
  B. A book where you write down your debts.
  C. A tool to create more debt.
  D. A place to keep your money that earns interest and can
     help avoid debt.

Answer: A savings account is a place to keep your money that earns interest over time. Having savings can help you avoid debt by giving you a cushion for unexpected expenses. (Answer D)

Feedback & tips: Try to save a small portion of your allowance or gift money regularly. Over time, this can grow and help you pay for big purchases without going into debt.

9. How can you avoid bad debt?

A. By spending all your money quickly.
B. By thinking carefully before borrowing and planning how
   to pay it back.
C. By borrowing as much money as possible.
D. By hiding your money.

Answer: You can avoid bad debt by thinking carefully before borrowing money, considering if you really need what you're borrowing for, and planning how you'll pay it back. (Answer B)

Feedback & tips: Always ask yourself, "Is this something I need or just want?" If it's just a want, it's better to save up for it instead of going into debt.

10. What should you do before taking on any debt?

A. Tell all your friends.
B. Research and understand the terms, and make sure you
   can afford to pay it back.
C. Spend all your current money.
D. Take a nap.

Answer: Before taking on any debt, research and understand the terms, like the interest rate and the payment schedule. Make sure you have the ability to pay it back on time. (Answer B)

Feedback & tips: Talking to a trusted adult about your plan to borrow money can give you a new perspective and help you make a smart decision about taking on debt.

Checklist for Healthy Credit Habits

- Pay bills on time, every time.
- Keep credit card balances well below your credit limits.
- Only apply for credit when absolutely necessary.
- Regularly check your credit report for accuracy (Have an adult help you with this.).
- Educate yourself on financial terms and rights as a borrower.

Building a positive relationship with credit doesn't have to be daunting. By understanding the basics of borrowing, distinguishing between good and bad debt, and adopting healthy credit habits early on, you can navigate the credit world like a pro. Remember, when used wisely, credit can be a powerful tool in achieving your financial goals.

5.2 THE DANGERS OF DEBT: WHY TO BE CAREFUL

Navigating the world of credit is like playing a game where the rules keep changing. It's exciting and can be rewarding, but there are pitfalls that can easily trip you up if you're not paying close attention. Understanding these pitfalls is crucial to playing the game smartly and keeping yourself on the path to financial well-being. Even if you're not currently borrowing money, understanding these dangers early on is important. By the time you're ready to venture out on your own, you'll have a head start, easily navigating past the money missteps that could trap your peers.

Compounding Interest on Debt

First, let's talk about how compounding interest can turn a small debt into a mountain. Unlike the interest in a savings account that works in your favor, interest on debt can quickly become your adversary. Imagine you owe money on a credit card. Each month, interest is added to your outstanding balance. The next month, you owe interest on the new balance, which now includes the previous month's interest. If you only make minimum payments, this cycle can make the amount you owe grow out of control.

Look at it this way, if your debt is a snowball rolling down a hill, compounding interest is the snow on the ground, making that ball bigger and bigger as it rolls.

Credit Card Traps

Credit cards, while useful, are loaded with traps for the unwary. The convenience and rewards they offer can be enticing, but they come with strings attached. It's never too early to learn about how they work.

- **Minimum payments**: Paying only the minimum payment due each month might seem like a relief for your wallet, but it's a slow drain on your financial health. This practice stretches your debt over years, inflating the total amount you pay because of compound interest.
- **High interest rates**: Credit cards most often have higher interest rates than other forms of debt. This rate can spike even higher if you miss a payment or your account is not in good standing.

- **Fees and penalties**: Late fees, annual fees, and charges for exceeding your credit limit can add up, eating into your budget.

Managing Existing Debt

Hopefully, you will avoid the stress of getting into debt while you're young because facing a pile of debt can feel like confronting a dragon in its den. With a strategic approach, however, you can tame the beast if you ever find yourself in this situation.

Here are some strategies:

- **Snowball method**: Focus on paying off your smallest debts first while making minimum payments on others. Once the smallest debt is cleared, move to the next smallest, and so on. This method can create momentum and a sense of achievement.
- **Avalanche method**: Alternatively, tackle debts with the highest interest rates first, regardless of the balance. This approach can save you money in the long run by reducing the amount of interest you'll pay.
- **Negotiating terms**: Reach out to your creditors to discuss more favorable repayment terms. You might be surprised at their willingness to work with you during tough times.

The Impact of Debt on Financial Goals

Debt doesn't just affect your current finances. It can also put future dreams on hold. Whether it's buying a home, traveling, or starting a business, debt can divert funds that would otherwise go toward these goals. It's like trying to fill a bucket with water when there's a hole in the bottom. No matter how much you pour in, you never seem to make progress.

- Think of your financial goals as the places you want to go on a map. Debt is the detour that takes you off your planned route, making it harder for you to get started on your journey.

Remember, debt isn't inherently bad. When used wisely, it's a tool that can help you achieve your goals. However, it demands respect and understanding. By recognizing the dangers of debt, you can confidently navigate the credit landscape, keeping your financial future bright and within reach.

5.3 CREDIT CARDS FOR KIDS: WHAT YOU NEED TO KNOW

Navigating the world of spending doesn't just involve knowing how much money you have in your piggy bank or savings account. In today's swipe-and-go society, understanding the difference between debit and credit cards is like learning to read a new language, one that can significantly impact your financial health if not understood properly.

Debit vs. Credit

So you've probably seen adults swiping or tapping their cards at stores without exchanging any cash. Most times, they're using one of two types of cards: debit or credit. Here's how they stack up against each other:

- Debit cards are direct lines to your bank account. Think of them as digital keys that unlock your own money vault. The cost is deducted from your account right away when you buy something. It's like having an invisible wallet that holds exactly what you have—no more, no less.
- Credit cards, however, are more like taking a loan for every purchase you make. The bank pays the store for you, and you agree to pay the bank back. The catch here is that you're not spending your money. You're spending the bank's money, and they'll charge you interest if you don't pay it back in time.

Getting the hang of using a debit card can be a great first step into the world of financial independence. It helps you practice spending only what you have, which is a golden rule for healthy finances.

Prepaid Credit Cards for Practice

Before diving into the ocean of credit, dipping your toes into a shallower pool might be wise. Enter prepaid credit cards. These are fantastic tools for learning the ropes of credit card management without the risk of sinking into debt. Here's why:

- You load prepaid cards with a set amount of money. Once it's gone, it's gone. You can't spend any more until you reload the card.
- Prepaid cards mimic the experience of using a credit card, including online purchases, without the danger of spending beyond your means.
- They're great for practicing budgeting. You can only spend what's on the card, making it easier to track and control your spending.

Understanding Credit Card Terms

Credit card agreements might seem like they're written in an ancient, mystical language. Here's a quick decoder for some of the terms you'll come across:

- APR (Annual Percentage Rate) shows the interest rate for a whole year, not just a month. It's how much the bank will charge you for borrowing their money.
- Your credit limit is the highest amount you can borrow on the card. Going over this limit usually results in extra fees.
- Late fees are what you pay if you miss the deadline for your monthly payment. These can add up and hurt your credit score, so always aim to pay on time.

By understanding these terms, you're better equipped to choose and use a credit card wisely, ensuring it becomes a tool for building your financial future, not a trap.

Safe Credit Practices

Keeping a few safety tips in mind can turn a credit card from a potential headache into a handy financial tool:

- Only use it for purchases you can afford. If you can't buy something with the cash you have now, think twice before charging it to your credit card.
- Always aim to pay off the full balance each month. This way, you avoid paying interest and you keep your credit score healthy.
- Keep track of your spending. Regularly check your account online to ensure you're not nearing your credit limit and to spot any suspicious activity.

- Know when to say no. Just because you have a credit limit doesn't mean you need to use it. Treat your credit card use with the same caution and consideration as spending physical cash.

Navigating credit successfully comes down to understanding the tools at your disposal, setting clear boundaries for yourself, and always aiming for practices that boost, rather than bust, your financial health. With these principles in hand, even the youngest spenders can start to build a credit history that opens doors to a healthy financial future.

5.4 BUILDING GOOD CREDIT: STARTING EARLY

Having a solid credit score is like holding a key that can unlock numerous doors in your future. It allows you to borrow money for big purchases later on, smooths the way to snagging that apartment you've been eyeing, and even sways potential employers who might check your credit as part of their hiring process. Let's explore some smart moves you can make to start building a strong credit foundation early on.

Co-Signed Accounts: A Team Effort

Getting into the credit game can be tricky without a history to show you're a safe bet. This is where having a co-signed account comes into play. It's like teaming up with someone who's already established good credit, such as a parent or guardian, to open an account. Their credit reputation gives lenders the confidence to take a chance on you. Using this account responsibly—think timely payments and smart spending—starts building your credit history. It's a partnership, so remember, any missteps not only affect your credit but also your co-signer's. Communication and responsibility are key.

Reporting Rent and Utility Payments: Everyday Credits

You might not know this, but the regular payments you make in the future for rent or utilities can also help build your credit history. Normally, these payments don't automatically show up on your credit report. However, services are available that can report these payments for you, turning your monthly rent and utility bills into opportunities to boost your credit score. It's like getting extra credit for homework you're already doing! Just make sure you're consistently making these payments on time because, like with any credit activity, late payments can ding your score.

Monitoring Credit: Keeping an Eye on Your Financial Pulse

As you get older and start building credit, staying informed about your credit status is crucial. Regularly checking your credit report keeps you up to date with your score and helps you make sure the information is accurate. Mistakes happen, and they can drag down your credit score if not corrected. Think of checking your credit report as doing a health check-up on your finances. You want to catch any errors early, from misreported late payments to accounts you don't recognize, which could be signs of identity theft. Most importantly, understanding the factors that influence your credit score gives you insights into how to improve it over time.

- Start by checking your credit report annually. It's free and doesn't affect your score.
- If you spot errors, report them immediately to the credit bureau for correction.

- Watching your credit score improve can be motivating, showing you the direct impact of your financial habits.

Building good credit is like a marathon, not a sprint. It requires patience, consistency, and smart habits. Remember, your credit score reflects your financial habits over time. By being responsible with a co-signed account, ensuring your regular payments are counted toward your credit history, and keeping a close watch on your credit report, you're laying a strong foundation for your financial future. These steps might seem small, but they're mighty in their ability to shape your credit journey positively.

As we wrap up this chapter, think of building good credit as planting a garden. It takes time, care, and a bit of daily attention, but the rewards—access to loans, better interest rates, and more financial opportunities—are well worth the effort. Keep nurturing your financial garden, and you'll be amazed at how it grows. Now, let's turn the page and discover more strategies for financial success.

YOUR REVIEW CAN SPARK A FINANCIAL REVOLUTION

Be the Hero in Someone's Financial Journey

"Every penny saved is a step towards a brighter future."

A TWIST ON BENJAMIN FRANKLIN.

Hey there, amazing young minds and the guardians of our future! Have you ever imagined turning your pocket money into a treasure chest, or better yet, becoming a financial superhero for someone just like you? Well, buckle up, because that's exactly the kind of adventure we're on with "The Ultimate Guide to Financial Literacy for Kids" by Money Mentor Publications.

Now, I've got a super important mission for you, should you choose to accept it.

Would you believe me if I told you that you could light up someone else's path to financial wisdom with just a few taps and a sprinkle of your thoughts? It's true! Like you, countless young adventurers are out there, eager to learn the secrets of saving, spending wisely, and growing their money trees. But here's the thing - they might not know where to start or which guide to trust on this thrilling journey.

This is where your superpowers come into play. Believe it or not, your words have the power to launch a thousand ships... or in this case, kickstart a thousand financial journeys!

Here's my heart-to-heart ask, from one bright spark to another:

Please take a moment to share your thoughts and leave this book a review.

Think of it as dropping a message in a bottle into the vast ocean of the internet. Your review could be the beacon that guides another young navigator to safe financial shores. And guess what? It won't cost you a dime, just a minute of your time, but the impact could be priceless.

Here's how you can unleash your superpower:

1. Grab your gadget and scan the QR code below.
2. Share your journey with "The Ultimate Guide to Financial Literacy for Kids".

https://www.amazon.com/review/create-review/?asin=
B0CZDGZGFG

If the thought of helping someone find their way makes your heart do a happy dance, then you, my friend, are a true hero. Welcome to the league of extraordinary financial wizards!

Thank you from every corner of my heart (and wallet). Now, let's dive back into our treasure trove of tips and tricks.

- Your biggest cheerleader, Money Mentor Publications

CHAPTER 6
DIGITAL DOLLARS AND SENSE: NAVIGATING FINANCE IN THE TECH AGE

Think of a world where your piggy bank gets smarter every day, learning the best ways to guard and grow your money. Now imagine this piggy bank isn't made of porcelain or plastic but bytes and pixels living inside your smartphone or tablet. Welcome to the modern era of managing money, where technology is not just an add-on to your financial journey, it's the vehicle driving you forward. In this chapter, we dive into the digital tools that make handling money easier and more fun.

First, let's tackle some tools revolutionizing how kids (and adults) think about and manage their finances: budgeting apps.

6.1 BUDGETING APPS FOR KIDS: TECH-SAVVY SAVING

The Role of Technology in Finance

When your parents were young, they kept track of their money by jotting down notes in a diary or trying to memorize what they spent at the candy store. Those days are fading fast, thanks to technology. Now apps can do the heavy lifting, tracking every dollar earned from mowing lawns or every penny saved for that new video game. They can even categorize your spending automatically, showing you where your money goes in colorful charts and graphs. It's like having a financial advisor in your pocket, one that's fun and friendly.

Top Budgeting Apps for Kids

- **Allowance & Chores Bot**: Imagine an app that helps you manage your chores and allowance all in one place. This app tracks the tasks you've completed and shows your earnings and spending. It's like a digital ledger that's easy to follow, which makes it perfect for keeping an eye on your financial goals.
- **GoHenry**: With features designed to teach money management through real-life experience, this app comes with a debit card just for kids. Parents control where and how the card can be used, making it a safe way to practice spending and saving in the digital world.
- **Bankaroo**: Created by a kid for kids, this app is all about making finance fun. It uses virtual money to help track savings goals, spending, and even charitable giving. It's a great first step into the world of budgeting without having to use real money.

Privacy and Security

With great power comes great responsibility, especially when that power is in an app. Using financial apps means sharing some personal information, which is why it's critical to understand privacy and security. Always:

- Ask a parent to help you check the app's privacy policy to see how your information is used and protected.
- Use strong passwords and never share them.
- Regularly review transactions and talk to a parent if anything looks off.

Remember, keeping your digital dollars safe is as important as protecting cash in a wallet.

Engaging With Parents

Don't fly solo on your financial voyage. These apps are an excellent way for you and your parents to talk about money matters together. Discussing savings goals, spending limits, and even charitable giving can turn into a family affair, making money management a shared adventure.

- Schedule regular check-ins to go over the app together. Discuss what you've learned and any adjustments you might want to make to your budget or savings goals.
- Use the app as a conversation starter for bigger financial discussions, like saving for college or understanding credit.

Technology has transformed the way we interact with money, making it more accessible, understandable, and engaging than ever before. With the right tools and a bit of curiosity, diving into the world of finance becomes an adventure, not a chore. As we continue to explore the digital world of money management, remember that these tools are here to serve you, helping to sculpt a financial future that's bright, informed, and full of potential.

6.2 CREATING A FINANCIAL JOURNAL: TRACKING YOUR MONEY

Imagine having a magic book that remembers where every cent of your allowance went and shows you how to make smarter money moves in the future. This is what happens when you start keeping a financial journal. It's your personal finance story, written by you, filled with insights into your spending habits and progress toward your goals.

Benefits of Journaling

A financial journal acts as your money mirror, reflecting back on your spending behaviors, saving patterns, and the journey toward your financial goals. It can highlight habits you didn't know you had, like that sneaky tendency to splurge on snacks after school. From putting pen to paper or tapping those keys, you start to see patterns, both good and bad. This awareness is the first step toward making change. Plus, recording your victories, no matter how small, can boost your motivation to keep going.

- **Insight**: Discover patterns in your spending and savings that you might not see otherwise.
- **Accountability**: Writing down your goals and keeping track of your progress keeps you accountable.
- **Motivation**: Celebrating your successes, big and small, keeps the motivation fire burning.

What to Track

Your financial journal can be as unique as you are, but there are a few key elements worth keeping tabs on:

- **Income**: This could be your allowance, money from odd jobs, or birthday cash. Knowing what money is coming in is crucial.
- **Expenses**: Track where your money's going, from the necessary (school supplies) to the fun (movies with friends).
- **Savings**: Keep a record of what you're saving for and how much you've tucked away. Watching this number grow can be super satisfying.
- **Financial goals**: Write down your goals, both short-term (a new game, for instance) and long-term (saving for a car). Seeing them in black and white makes them feel more achievable.

Journaling Methods

The beauty of a financial journal is that it can be anything you want it to be. Here are a couple of ways to get started:

- **Pen and paper**: There's something special about writing things down the old-fashioned way. A dedicated notebook where you write down your financial observations can be a tangible reminder of your money journey. Plus, you can get creative with colored pens and stickers to make it your own.
- **Digital journaling**: If you're more tech-inclined, numerous apps and software can serve as your digital journal. They offer the convenience of having your financial info at your fingertips, often with added features like automatic categorization and visual charts. Work with a parent to choose the one that would work best for you, and make sure to back up your data to avoid losing your valuable insights.

Review and Reflect

The real power of a financial journal lies in regularly sitting down to review and reflect on what you've written. This helps you recognize where you can improve and acknowledge what you're doing right. Set aside a time each week to go through your journal. Ask yourself:

- What was my biggest financial win this week?
- Did I make any impulse purchases? What led to them?
- How am I progressing toward my financial goals?
- What can I do differently next week to improve?

This practice lets you keep track of numbers and understand the why behind your financial decisions. It turns your journal into a tool for growth, helping you make smarter choices in the future.

Keeping a financial journal is like drawing your own map in the treasure hunt of personal finance. It guides you through the forests of spending, over the mountains of saving, and toward the goals you've set for yourself. With every entry, you're writing the story of your financial journey, one page at a time.

6.3 ONLINE BANKING BASICS FOR THE YOUNG SAVER

Gone are the days when saving meant stuffing crumpled notes and jingling coins into an old, dusty piggy bank. The banking world has taken a giant leap into the digital realm, making managing your money just a click or tap away. But what exactly is online banking, and how does it work? Think of it as your digital wallet, always ready, always accessible, wherever you have access to a phone or tablet.

Online Banking Simplified

Online banking lets you handle your money without visiting a physical bank. Imagine being able to check how much money you have, move some of it to a friend as a birthday gift, or save a chunk of it for that dream hoverboard—all from your device. It's banking at your fingertips, on your schedule and not the bank's.

Features of Online Banking

Diving a bit deeper, online banking comes with a lot of features designed to make your life easier. Here are a few you might find super handy:

- **Checking your balance**: Know exactly how much money you have at any moment. It's like having a financial mirror that reflects your current money situation, helping you make informed spending decisions.
- **Money transfers**: Want to split the cost of a gift or pay back a friend? Online banking lets you transfer money in a snap, often without any fees, especially if the recipient is with the same bank.
- **Mobile deposits**: Did you receive a check for your birthday? No need to run to the bank. Just take a picture with your phone and deposit it through your banking app. Magic? Almost.
- **Bill payments**: Though more relevant for adults, it's cool to know that bills can be paid directly through online banking.

Safety Tips for Online Banking

As always, having all this power comes with responsibility, especially when it comes to keeping your digital dollars safe. Here are some golden rules for secure online banking:

- **Strong passwords**: Your first line of defense. Mix letters, numbers, and special characters to create a password that's tough to crack.
- **Phishing scam awareness**: Scammers might try to trick you into giving them your banking info. Your bank will *never* ask for your password or PIN via email or text. If someone is asking, they're trying to trick you.
- **Public Wi-Fi caution**: Using public Wi-Fi for banking is like leaving your wallet open on a park bench. If you need to bank on the go, use your data plan or a secure VPN.
- **Log out after every session**: Just like you wouldn't leave your house door open when you leave, always log out of your banking app when you're done.

The Future of Banking

Peering into the crystal ball of banking, we see a world where cryptocurrencies and blockchain technology play bigger roles.

- Cryptocurrencies are like special online coins that are kept safe with secret codes. They don't belong to any bank or country. You might know names like Bitcoin or Ethereum. These special coins could change the way we use and think about our allowance or savings in the future.
- Blockchain technology is the backbone of cryptocurrencies. It's a system of recording information in a way that makes it

difficult or impossible to change or cheat. It could make banking even more secure and transparent in the future.

Online banking is more than just a convenience, it's a shift in how we interact with money, blending security with accessibility. As banking continues evolving with advancements like cryptocurrencies and blockchain, staying informed and cautious ensures your digital financial journey is exciting and safe. Let's take a deeper dive, shall we?

6.4 THE FUTURE OF MONEY: DIGITAL CURRENCIES AND KIDS

Imagine a world where money isn't something you hold in your hand. Instead, it's a digital code on your computer or phone. This isn't out of a sci-fi movie, it's the reality of digital currencies, also known as cryptocurrencies. Unlike the dollars or coins in your pocket, digital currencies aren't printed or minted by governments. They exist entirely online and are created and held electronically.

Breaking Down Digital Currencies

At their core, digital currencies are a form of money that's available only in digital or electronic form. Bitcoin, the first and most well-known cryptocurrency, popped onto the scene in 2009, opening the floodgates to a whole new way of thinking about money. Cryptocurrencies use blockchain, which is like a big online notebook that keeps track of everyone's digital coin trades without needing a bank. It's like if you traded stickers directly with your friends without anyone else needing to check or approve the trade. This makes it a system where people can exchange digital coins directly with each other.

Using Digital Money

You might wonder how digital currencies fit into your life as a kid. While you're not likely to invest in Bitcoin anytime soon, you're already encountering digital money in different forms:

- **Online gaming currencies**: Many online games have their own form of currency, like Robux in Roblox or V-Bucks in Fortnite. These virtual currencies are used to buy in-game items or upgrades and are a simple, kid-friendly introduction to digital money.
- **Gift cards**: Have you ever received a digital gift card? It's another form of digital currency. You use a code to redeem the card online, exchanging it for goods or services without touching physical money.

Risks and Considerations

While digital currencies offer exciting possibilities, they come with their own set of challenges:

- **Volatility**: Volatility means something can change quickly and unpredictably. That means the value of cryptocurrencies can vary greatly from one day to the next. This unpredictability makes them a risky investment because their worth can significantly increase or decrease quickly.
- **Understanding value**: Grasping the concept of digital money's value can be tricky since it's not something you can physically see or touch. It's important to learn how to equate digital currencies with real-world money to understand what you're spending or potentially earning.

Financial Literacy in a Digital Age

As the world becomes more digital, financial literacy means you need to know about more than counting cash or saving in a bank. You have to navigate the digital financial landscape. Understanding digital currencies and how they operate is becoming an essential skill. You need to know how to do it and be aware of the risks, the security measures needed to protect digital assets, and the ethical considerations of using such technologies.

- **Embrace curiosity**: Dive into learning about digital currencies and blockchain technology. The more you know, the better prepared you'll be for the financial world of tomorrow.
- **Stay cautious**: While exploring digital money, always remember the importance of security. Protecting your digital wallet is as crucial as safeguarding physical money.
- **Think ahead**: As you save and plan for the future, consider how digital currencies might play a role in your financial strategies. The landscape of money and investment is evolving, and staying informed will keep you ahead of the curve.

In wrapping up this glimpse into the future of money, it's clear that the financial world kids are growing into is very different from previous generations. Digital currencies, with their blend of technology and finance, are paving new roads for transactions, savings, and investments. Understanding these digital assets, their benefits, and their risks is crucial for anyone looking to successfully navigate tomorrow's financial waters. As we move forward, keep an open mind, stay informed, and approach the digital financial realm with both enthusiasm and caution. This balance will serve you well as you step into the future of money equipped with the knowledge and skills to thrive in an increasingly digital world. Now, let's turn the page, ready to tackle new adventures in personal finance.

Chapter 6 Review Activity

```
R S N B T Z X B J N S G T C D Y C T C W Z X
W K O D J L Y R S O T Q P R E D K Q Y O G I
G R L C X A P F A P P S Z Y A U R T J Y G B
P L Y F T U U D A U N X H P Y N I P C G E L
K M V Q I S E Y P C U C P T Q R S V Z P X O
R P P V N N W Q A G V E G O U D B F V K G C
B D I G I T A L D E X N P C P X Q J E D P K
F I N A N C E N Y F I D E U Q C J G U R A C
C U T G U X B L C K D S H R Y Z P E D S S H
W B U C W F N R N I C N M R Y R U B S Q S A
N T H G O Q J A V Z A E R E V E E O E P W I
R F D Q N I B H S F L L T N I R B M O N O N
C Q Z I I E N U A C P N L C B R S X E Q R A
U K R R N W U T V A M H Y I C N Y L I D D S
Y U L I G E Y A I D M J I E T K X Y I A S Y
A N L O N I J N N U S L Z S I E F N K N N C
N N U R H D G S G V L K N Q H F R O E G E C
O U M H M U F I S I H D Y Z D I K A M Q W C
Y P E T M D G A G O H E N R Y Y N O C I D S
I P V B X A M V Z Q G E E F C R J G I Y X I
Q G D Y K T Z J W R Q R T S X V I A M D C T
V C L F D E C X Y Y Q P W W C Y W I U V R Q
```

Digital	Finance	Apps
Savings	GoHenry	Security
Cryptocurrencies	Blockchain	Online Banking
Transfers	Passwords	Bitcoin
Financial Literacy	Phishing	

Answer Key on Page 162

CHAPTER 7
NAVIGATING MONEY MISSTEPS

I magine waking up one morning to find that your favorite game, which used to cost 10 coins, now costs 20 coins. Frustrating, right? It's a bit like life. Sometimes, things don't go as planned, especially when it comes to managing our money. This chapter is your map for dodging financial pitfalls and making smarter moves with your money. Money missteps are like tripping over a rake in the yard. They're bound to happen, but with some care, you can avoid a cartoonish faceplant.

7.1 COMMON MONEY BLUNDERS KIDS MAKE

Overspending on Trends

It's hard not to want the latest sneakers or the newest phone everyone's talking about. But constantly chasing trends can lead to spending more money than you have. Remember, trends come and go. Today's must-have item can quickly become tomorrow's garage sale bargain. So, before you spend, ask yourself, "Will I still use this a month from now?" If the answer is "probably not," you might want to rethink that purchase.

Neglecting to Save

Sometimes, saving money feels like a chore, especially when there's something shiny and new catching your eye. But not stashing away part of your allowance or birthday money can leave you high and dry when you really need or want something. Start small, even a little bit saved regularly can add up over time. Think of saving as paying your future self. It's like planting a seed that eventually grows into a money tree you can harvest later.

Giving In to Peer Pressure

We've all been there. Your friend shows off a new gadget, and suddenly, you feel like you need one, too, even if it means spending all your savings. Peer pressure is tough, but remember, true friends won't judge you based on what you have or don't have. It's okay to say no or suggest a more budget-friendly activity. Your wallet will thank you.

Here's a toolkit of responses that can help you stand your ground when faced with peer pressure, especially regarding spending money. Try these ready-to-use scripts:

When Friends Want You to Buy Expensive Things

- Response: "I'm saving up for something special, so I can't join in on buying that right now."

When Everyone is Getting the Latest Gadget

- Response: "It looks cool, but my old one still works fine. I'd rather save my money for something else."

When Being Teased for Not Having Brand-Name Items

- Response: "Brands don't really matter to me. I like what I have, and that's enough."

When Encouraged to Spend All Your Money at Once

- Response: "I'm learning to manage my money better. Part of that is not spending it all in one place."

When Invited to Expensive Outings

- Response: "That sounds fun, but it's a bit too pricey for me. Can we do something less expensive instead?"

When Pressured to Lend Money

- Response: "I'm really careful about where my money goes. I can't lend it out, but I'm here to help you figure out another solution."

When Everyone Wants to Pool Money for a Big Purchase

- Response: "I'm on a tight budget and have to pass this time. Maybe next time we can plan something that fits everyone's budget."

When Friends Mock You for Budgeting

- Response: "Budgeting helps me keep track of my money and spend it on things I really want or need. I think it's pretty smart."

When Being Called Cheap for Not Spending Freely

- Response: "I prefer to think of it as being smart with my money. Saving now means I can enjoy something even better later."

When Tempted to Buy Just to Fit In

- Response: "I'd rather save my money for things I'm truly excited about, not just to keep up with everyone else."

Practicing these scripts can help you feel more prepared and secure in your decisions when faced with financial peer pressure.

Forgetting About Future Needs

Thinking ahead isn't just for grown-ups. Whether it's saving for a new game that's coming out in six months or setting aside money for a school trip, planning for future expenses ensures you won't be caught off guard. It's like packing an umbrella on a cloudy day. You might not need it, but you'll be glad to have it if it rains.

- Reflection: What's one thing you wish you had saved for but didn't? How would saving for it have made a difference? As you write, think about the impact of saving on achieving your goals.

Navigating money missteps isn't going to be perfect, but you'll learn, adjust, and make smarter decisions next time. Whether you've splurged on a fleeting trend, forgotten to feed your piggy bank, caved to the call of the crowd, or overlooked future needs, each mistake is a stepping stone to becoming more financially savvy. Remember, the best financial plan is the one that works for you, grows with you, and helps you dodge those metaphorical rakes in the yard of life.

7.2 LESSONS FROM MONEY MISTAKES: GROWING SMARTER

Mistakes, especially those involving money, often feel like stumbling blocks. Yet they're hidden gems packed with insights ready to be uncovered. This part of our adventure shines a light on the silver linings found in financial missteps, showcasing how they can sculpt us into more savvy money managers.

Learning From Experience

Diving into tales where kids faced financial oops moments can be enlightening. Picture Zack, who once spent his entire summer savings on a fancy remote-controlled car, only to find it gathering dust a week later. The initial thrill faded, leaving Zack with a valuable lesson: Instant gratification often leads to lasting regret. Or consider Maya, who, in a bid to keep up appearances, bought trendy sneakers that plunged her savings into the red—they cost more than she had saved. The experience taught her the importance of living within her means, setting her on a path to more mindful spending.

These narratives aren't just stories. They're windows into the consequences of our choices, teaching us to pause and ponder before making similar decisions.

The Role of Setbacks

Encountering a financial setback can feel like hitting a roadblock on your path to saving glory. Yet it's in these moments that growth sprouts. Each setback, be it an impulsive buy that empties your wallet or a forgotten savings goal, is a step toward better financial habits. Through these experiences, we learn resilience, discovering that bouncing back with a smarter plan is always possible. This resilience builds a financial backbone sturdy enough to support smarter decisions in the future.

Asking for Advice

When money matters get confusing, asking for help can make things a lot clearer. Sometimes, kids might be scared to ask questions because they don't want to be judged for making mistakes. But talking to parents, teachers, or someone else who knows a lot about money can help you see things you didn't notice before. These talks can make the tricky parts of dealing with money easier to understand. They're a chance to learn from others who have been through their own money adventures and can guide you on what to do.

- Have a family meeting about money every month. Talk about what you hope to do with your money, any problems you've had, and what you've done well.
- Talk in class about a money choice you made recently. Ask your friends and teacher what they think and if they have any other ideas on what you could do.
- If you can, meet with a money expert to make plans. They can help you figure out how to reach your money goals.

Adapting and Adjusting

The financial landscape is ever-changing, much like the seasons. A strategy that worked brilliantly last year might not fit this year's goals or challenges. This fluidity demands flexibility, the willingness to tweak and refine your financial plan to ensure it remains aligned with your evolving needs and aspirations. It's about staying dynamic, ready to adjust sails when the financial winds shift. This adaptability ensures that your money management strategies grow with you, always reflecting your current reality and future dreams.

- Regularly review your financial goals, asking if they still meet your aspirations.
- Experiment with different saving techniques or budgeting apps to find what works best for you.
- Reflect on past financial mistakes, considering how different strategies could prevent similar outcomes.

In essence, the journey through financial missteps to smarter money management is paved with lessons waiting to be learned. Each stumble, each fall, is a chance to rise stronger, equipped with newfound wisdom. Through these experiences, we become not just wise spenders and savers but also resilient navigators of our financial futures.

7.3 THE IMPORTANCE OF FINANCIAL DISCIPLINE

In the world of money matters, being disciplined is like having a superpower. It's the key to unlocking your goals, one saved coin at a time. But what does it really mean to be financially disciplined? Think of it as making decisions today that will make you proud tomorrow. It's about choosing to save instead of spend, and planning instead of splurging.

What is Financial Discipline?

Financial discipline is the practice of making decisions about your money that are in line with your long-term goals. It's not about never having fun or spending money; it's about knowing when and how to do so wisely. This might mean waiting a bit longer to buy that new game so you can keep your savings on track or choosing to do extra chores to earn more money before making a purchase. Essentially, it's learning how to control your impulses so they don't control you.

Building Self-Control

Gaining control over your spending and saving habits doesn't happen overnight. It's built through small, daily choices. Here are a few strategies to help you develop this important skill:

- **Pause before purchasing**: Give yourself a cooling-off period before buying something non-essential. Sometimes the urge to buy fades if you give it a little time.
- **Needs vs. wants list**: Keep a list of items you need versus things you want. Prioritize spending on your needs before your wants.
- **Visual reminders**: Place pictures of your savings goals around your room or set them as backgrounds on your devices. Seeing what you're saving for can help keep you focused.

Developing self-control is part practice, part patience. It's normal to slip up now and then. The key is to learn from those experiences and keep moving forward.

Setting and Sticking to Budgets

A budget is like a blueprint for your financial goals. It gives you a clear picture of where your money should go every month, helping you make the most of every dollar. Here are some ways to create and stick to a realistic budget:

- **Track your spending**: For a set period of time—say, a week or a month—write down everything you spend money on. This will give you a clear idea of where your money is going.
- **Categorize your expenses**: Divide your spending into categories like savings, essentials (food, clothes), and extras (games, outings).
- **Allocate wisely**: Based on your tracking, decide how much money to put into each category. Be realistic about your needs and consistent with your savings goals.

- **Review regularly**: At the end of each month, review your spending. Did you stick to your budget? Where could you improve? Adjust your budget as needed.

Remember, a budget doesn't restrict freedom. It's a tool that helps you achieve your financial goals while still enjoying life.

Delayed Gratification

Delayed gratification is a cornerstone of financial discipline. It's choosing to wait for a more significant reward instead of giving in to the temptation of immediate pleasure. Here's why it's worth practicing:

- **Bigger and better rewards**: Saving for a bigger goal often means the reward is much more satisfying than smaller impulse purchases.
- **Reduced buyer's remorse**: Waiting to make a purchase often leads to more thoughtful spending, reducing the chances of regretting your decisions later.
- **Increased financial stability**: Practicing delayed gratification helps you save more, spend less, and avoid debt, leading to a more stable financial future.

Learning to wait for what you want can be as simple as picking something you'd like to save for, and then slowly saving money until you can buy it. Each time you choose to save instead of spend, you're reinforcing the habit of delayed gratification.

Financial discipline might sound daunting, but it's really just making choices that align with your goals. It allows you to see the big picture and understand that the best rewards are often those we work hard for and wait patiently to achieve. Every time you make a smart choice with your money, you're not just saving, you're creating a base for a future where you can achieve your money goals and make your dreams come true, one smart step at a time.

7.4 ASKING FOR HELP: WHEN TO TALK TO ADULTS ABOUT MONEY

Money talks can sometimes feel like trying to understand a foreign language. That's okay, though. Everyone starts somewhere, and asking questions is how we learn and grow. Imagine cracking open a secret code with the help of those who've been decoding it for years. That's what talking about money with adults can feel like—unlocking secrets that make managing money easier and more effective.

Opening Up Conversations

Starting a conversation about money might seem hard, but it's like ripping off a band-aid. The initial hesitation quickly gives way to relief once you dive in. Trusted adults in your life—be it parents, older siblings, or family friends—have a treasure trove of experiences. They've likely faced money challenges and triumphs and can share wisdom you won't find in any textbook. Try asking them about their first savings goal or what they wish they knew about money when they were your age. You'll be surprised at how much you can learn from their stories.

Learning From Others

There's a saying that wisdom is learning from the mistakes of others. Your family, teachers, and even neighbors have all navigated their financial waters, sometimes smoothly, other times not so much. Their journeys are resources for you. Did your aunt invest in something that didn't pan out? What did she learn? Has a teacher ever shared a story about a financial blunder? These real-life lessons are invaluable. They give you the knowledge to make informed decisions and avoid similar pitfalls.

Seeking Professional Advice

Sometimes you might need more than just family wisdom, especially when you're planning for big goals like college. This is where financial advisors can be game-changers. Think of them as guides in the complex world of money management. They can help you understand saving options, the magic of compound interest, and how to start investing wisely, even with a small amount. If your family has a financial advisor, ask if you can join a meeting. Many banks and community centers also offer financial planning sessions. They're like having a coach for your money, helping you train to reach your financial fitness goals.

Resources for Learning

The great news is that more resources are available to you than ever. Websites and apps can make learning about money management both fun and engaging. Here are a few to get you started:

- Websites like Biz Kid$ offer a wealth of information, interactive games, and real-life stories of kids and money.
- Apps like Bankaroo for kids and teens offer a hands-on approach to managing virtual money, teaching valuable skills in a controlled environment.

Dip your toes into these resources. Each one has something unique to offer, from beginning concepts to advanced strategies, all tailored to help you navigate your financial journey.

As we wrap up this exploration into the world of money management, remember it's okay to ask for help. Whether it's opening up to trusted adults, learning from their experiences, seeking professional advice, or exploring online resources, every step you take builds your understanding and confidence in handling money. These conversations equip you with the tools to make informed decisions, set and achieve goals, and navigate the financial challenges and opportunities that lie ahead. Now, with a solid grasp of money management basics and the wisdom gleaned from those around you, you're ready to move forward, making smarter financial choices that pave the way to a bright and prosperous future.

CHAPTER 8
THE CLEAR GLASS: SEEING THROUGH MONEY MATTERS

I magine walking into a room full of windows. Some windows reveal a very clear picture, while others are cracked or dirty. The clear windows help you see where to go to avoid obstacles or wrong paths, while the cracked or dirty ones block your path. This is similar to being transparent in money matters. The clearer we are about our financial dealings, the easier it is to avoid problems like scams or dishonesty.

Transparency is the cornerstone of trust, especially when handling money. Whether within personal finance or the wider business world, being open about financial transactions and decisions can build bridges of trust. Yet the fog of scams and the allure of easy gains can sometimes cloud our judgment. Here's how to keep your financial dealings as transparent as those clear windows so you can always see the way forward.

8.1 UNDERSTANDING FINANCIAL TRANSPARENCY

Financial transparency means keeping the curtains open on all your money dealings. It means making sure everything from your savings progress to your spending habits is visible, not just to you but also to anyone else involved, like parents or financial advisors. In businesses, it involves openly sharing financial reports and operations with stakeholders.

Financial transparency is important because it builds trust. When people can see where their money is going or how a business operates financially, it fosters confidence and security. It clears up suspicion and doubt, making financial relationships smoother and more straightforward.

Honesty With Money

Being honest about money, whether with yourself, your family, or in any financial transaction, is a key part of transparency. This means:

- **Paying what you owe**: Paying back any money you borrow from friends or family on time shows you are trustworthy and honest.
- **Full disclosure**: When you borrow or lend money, it's important to be clear about how much you have, and how you'll either pay it back or be paid back. Talking about how much extra money (interest) needs to be paid, how and when the money will be returned, and if there are any money problems right from the start helps avoid confusion and builds trust.

Teaching Transparency

For parents and educators, instilling the value of transparency in young minds is crucial. It paves the way for responsible and trust-worthy financial behaviors in the future. Here's how to make it part of everyday learning:

- **Be an open book**: Share your financial decisions, the reasoning behind them, and their outcomes with your kids. Let them in on the process, whether it's about budgeting for groceries or choosing a savings account.
- **Encourage questions**: Foster an environment where asking about money matters is okay. Talk about how credit cards work or why we pay taxes, providing clear, honest answers that demystify financial concepts.
- **Lead by example**: Practice what you preach. Let your kids see you reviewing bills, discussing finances openly with your partner, or researching before making an investment. Actions often speak louder than words.

8.2 FINANCIAL SCAMS: STAYING SAFE AND SMART

These days, pocket money can be sent with a click and piggy banks are getting smart, and the shadows of financial scams loom larger and sneakier than ever. From the age-old bait of prize-winning emails to the more sophisticated online identity thefts, scams have evolved, preying on the internet's uninformed and overly trusting souls.

Overview of Common Financial Scams

Scams are like the chameleons of the financial world. They blend in, adapting to the latest trends and technologies to catch you off guard. Young folks and adults alike might find themselves facing:

- **Phishing emails and messages**: These trick you into giving away personal info under the guise of legitimate requests from banks or familiar services.
- **Fake online stores**: Ever stumbled upon a sale too good to ignore? Some of these are fronts for collecting payment details without delivering the goods.
- **Investment fraud**: Offers promising you'll make lots of money with little to no risk might lead you down a path where the only thing growing is the scammer's wallet.
- **Identity theft**: A scary scenario where someone steals your personal information and then uses it to steal your money or commit other crimes, leaving you to untangle the mess.

Here are some red flags to watch for:

1. **Pressure to act quickly**: Scammers often create a sense of urgency, pushing you to make decisions on the spot without giving you time to think or consult others.
2. **Requests for personal or financial information**: Be cautious if you're asked for sensitive details like your bank account numbers, Social Security number, or login credentials for online accounts. No responsible company asks for your password in an email.
3. **Unsolicited contact**: Receiving unexpected calls, emails, or messages, especially from unknown sources or pretending to be from a real organization, can be a scam attempt.

4. **Too good to be true offers**: Promises of high returns with no risk, winning a contest you didn't enter, or deals that seem too good to be true are classic scam tactics.

5. **Payment requests via unusual methods**: Scammers often ask for payments through wire transfers, prepaid debit cards, gift cards, or cryptocurrencies, which are hard to trace and recover.

6. **Vague details and lack of transparency**: If the person or organization is vague about who they are, where they are located, or details of the offer, that's a red flag telling you to check with an adult before continuing.

7. **Spelling and grammar errors**: Professional organizations usually have communications checked for errors, so poorly written emails or messages can be a sign of a scam.

8. **Mismatched email addresses or URLs**: If the email address or link doesn't match the supposed organization's official domain, it could be a phishing attempt.

9. **Asking to keep transactions a secret**: Scammers might ask you not to tell anyone about the deal, aiming to isolate you from advice that could reveal the scam.

10. **Manipulation tactics**: Emotional manipulation, such as creating fear (e.g., claiming you'll be arrested for unpaid taxes) or offering sympathy or friendship, is often used to exploit victims.

Protecting Personal Information

The key to keeping scammers at bay is to treat your personal and financial information like the crown jewels—keep them under lock and key. Here are some ways to stay safe:

- **Strong passwords**: Use a mix of letters, numbers, and symbols that are hard to guess. Have a parent help you keep track of them all.
- **Privacy settings**: On social media, lock your profiles. The less strangers know about you, the better.
- **Secure connections**: Public Wi-Fi can be a hacker's playground. Avoid accessing sensitive accounts when connected to them.
- **Shred and secure**: Old-fashioned paper can still hold valuable info. Shred documents you don't need and keep important ones in a safe place.

Critical Thinking

If your gut says something's fishy, it probably is. Scammers love to create a sense of urgency or excitement to cloud your judgment. Slow down and think.

- **Question everything**: Why would your bank email you asking for your password? Can that online investment really guarantee high returns with no risk?
- **Research**: A quick internet search can reveal if others have encountered similar scams.
- **Talk about it**: Sometimes just discussing a suspicious offer with someone else can highlight its absurdity.

Reporting and Recovery

So you've spotted a scam or, worse, fallen for one. It's not the end of the world, but action is needed:

- **Report it**: Have a parent help you. Banks, social media platforms, and government agencies have channels for reporting fraud. They can also offer guidance on your next steps.
- **Change passwords**: If your information might have been compromised, change your passwords immediately.
- **Monitor your accounts**: Regularly check your bank account and credit report for any unusual activity.
- **Learn from it**: Every scam faced is a lesson learned. Share your experience to help protect others.

In every tale of heroes and villains, knowledge is power. By staying informed about the types of scams out there, keeping your personal and financial information safe, thinking critically, and knowing how to react if things go bad, you're not just protecting your money but building a fortress around your financial future. Now, let's move forward to the next chapter, ready to take on the exciting financial adventures ahead.

8.3 FINANCIAL HONESTY QUIZ

Try this fun, interactive quiz that tests your knowledge on financial transparency, covering topics like recognizing scams, the importance of honesty in money dealings, and ways to maintain financial integrity. Each question comes with feedback to help reinforce learning.

Question 1: What should you do if a stranger online asks for your parent's bank account details to give you a free video game?

> A. Give them the details.
> B. Ignore the request.
> C. Ask for two video games instead.
> D. Tell a trusted adult about it.

Feedback: Answer D. Great choice! If someone you don't know asks for private information, you should always tell a trusted adult. Scammers often use tricks like this to steal money.

Question 2: Why is it important to tell the truth when talking about how much allowance you have?

A. It makes you more popular.
B. It helps build trust with others.
C. You get more allowance.
D. It's not that important.

Feedback: Answer B. Correct! Being honest about your money builds trust, and people will know they can rely on you to be truthful.

Question 3: If a friend lends you money to buy a toy, what's the best way to handle it?

A. Pay them back as promised.
B. Wait for them to forget about it.
C. Tell them you lost the money.
D. Buy them a gift instead.

Feedback: Answer A. Exactly right! Paying back money you owe shows you respect your friend and take your promises seriously.

Question 4: What is a scam?

A. A type of dance.
B. A trick to steal your money.
C. A new video game.
D. A financial advisor.

Feedback: Answer B. Spot on! A scam is a trick someone uses to steal money or information. Always be cautious and ask an adult if something seems suspicious.

Question 5: If you see an ad promising free money, what should you think?

    A. It's my lucky day!
    B. It might be a scam.
    C. I should click on it immediately.
    D. I should tell all my friends.

Feedback: Answer B. Well done! Offers of free money are usually too good to be true and could be scams. Always check with an adult before responding.

Question 6: Why is it important to discuss the details when borrowing or lending money with a friend?

    A. It's not really important.
    B. To make the conversation longer.
    C. To prevent misunderstandings and keep the friendship strong.
    D. To confuse everyone.

Feedback: Answer C. Absolutely! Discussing details like when you'll pay them back helps avoid any confusion and keeps your friendship healthy and happy.

Question 7: What should you do before making a deal or trade, like swapping toys with a friend?

    A. Talk about it clearly and agree on the details.
    B. Just go ahead and swap without talking.
    C. Make the trade secretly.
    D. Change your mind at the last minute.

Feedback: Answer A. Great job! Talking things over and agreeing on the details first makes sure both friends are happy and there are no surprises.

Question 8: How can you be financially transparent or completely honest with your parents about your allowance?

    A. Only tell them about what you save.
    B. Share how you plan to spend and save, and any mistakes you've made.
    C. Hide some of your spending.
    D. Spend it all quickly so there's nothing to tell.

Feedback: Answer B. That's the way! Being open with your parents about your money helps you learn and grow, and they can offer great advice and support.

Checklist for Transparent Financial Dealings

- Always research before investing or engaging in financial opportunities.
- Keep records of all transactions, big or small.
- Discuss financial decisions openly with family members or advisors.
- Regularly review your financial habits and goals, keeping an eye out for areas to improve transparency.
- Educate yourself and others about the dangers of scams and the importance of honesty in all financial matters.

In a world where financial dealings can sometimes feel like navigating a maze of mirrors, choosing transparency is like carrying a light that reveals the true path. It guides your way and illuminates the road for those following in your footsteps. By committing to clear, honest, and open financial practices, we can all contribute to a future where trust and integrity lead the way in personal finance and beyond.

CHAPTER 9
MONEY MAGIC: TRANSFORMING FINANCE WITH FUN AND GAMES

I magine you're at a magic show where the magician pulls a rabbit out of a hat, makes coins disappear, and then, with a flourish, turns those same coins into a shower of colorful paper money. What if I told you that you could perform your own kind of magic right at home, transforming how you think about and handle money, all while having a blast? Yes, you heard that right! This chapter is all about turning financial literacy into an exciting game, one that not only educates but entertains. From board games that mimic real-life financial situations to creating your very own game that teaches you the ropes of economics, we will explore how fun and finance can go hand in hand.

9.1 BOARD GAMES THAT TEACH FINANCIAL LITERACY

Educational Value of Board Games

Board games have an incredible ability to teach concepts that may be complex in a fun and engaging way. Think about it. When trying to conquer a game, you're not just focused on winning, you're learning strategies, making decisions, and sometimes even doing a bit of math. And when it comes to financial literacy, board games can be a gold mine. They can show you the importance of saving, the impact of investments, and the consequences of debt, all within the confines of a game board. Plus, they bring people together, sparking conversations about money that might not happen otherwise.

Popular Financial Board Games

Some board games are classics for a reason. They've been around for ages and are still as popular as ever. Here's why:

- **Monopoly**: This game is practically a rite of passage. You're getting a crash course in real estate and money management as you buy properties, pay rent, and manage your cash. The key takeaway? Investing wisely can make you rich, but overextend yourself, and you could go bankrupt.
- **The Game of Life**: Here you're navigating life's big financial milestones—college, career, child-rearing, home buying, and retirement. It's a vivid reminder that our choices, especially financial ones, steer our life's direction.
- **Payday**: Living from paycheck to paycheck? Payday puts you in this scenario, teaching you to budget your monthly

income to cover bills and unexpected expenses and save a bit, too.

- **Cashflow**: Created by financial guru Robert Kiyosaki, it challenges players to get out of the rat race and onto the fast track, where their wealth can grow.

Creating Your Own Financial Board Game

Now, for the ultimate challenge: making your own board game. Why not turn what you've learned about earning, spending, saving, and investing into a game? You could design a game where players have to make money last through the month, invest in businesses, or save for retirement. The sky's the limit. Not only does this flex your creative muscles, but it also deepens your understanding of financial concepts. And who knows? Your game could become the next family favorite, teaching and entertaining players for generations to come.

Learning Through Competition

There's something about a little friendly competition that makes any game more thrilling. When you're competing, you're more focused, engaged, and determined to win. In the context of financial board games, this competition can simulate real-life financial decision-making and risk-taking. You could read about the stock market, but it's more fun to watch your investment in GameStop soar or plummet in a game, feeling that rush of excitement or pang of disappointment. This hands-on experience, even in a simulated environment, can prepare you for the ups and downs of real-world finances.

So grab a board game or start brainstorming your own, and dive into the world of financial literacy. Remember, the goal isn't just to win the game but to uncover hidden financial strategies and lessons, making you a better player and a smarter financial thinker.

9.2 FUN MONEY CHALLENGES FOR FAMILIES

Gather around, family! It's time to put a spin on our usual routines and add a sprinkle of excitement to our financial habits. Who said managing money had to be all spreadsheets and no play? Let's dive into some family-friendly challenges that will not only bring us closer but also teach us valuable lessons about money.

Saving Challenge

Imagine a treasure chest where every family member contributes, with eyes on a prize that benefits everyone. Sounds like an adventure, doesn't it? Here's the plan: We pick a goal that gets everyone pumped —maybe a new gaming console or a weekend getaway. Each week, we all chip in an agreed amount into our family treasure chest (a.k.a. savings jar). Watching our collective treasure grow brings a sense of teamwork and anticipation. The best part? Reaching our goal and celebrating together, knowing we all played a part in achieving it.

Tips for success:

- Set a visible savings jar in a common area to remind and motivate everyone.
- Keep track of contributions with a colorful chart on the fridge.
- Encourage extra contributions by offering small, fun incentives, like choosing the next family movie night film.

Spending Diary

Let's turn into financial detectives for one week and track where our money goes. Everyone gets a notebook to write down their spending, no matter how small. At the end of the week, we'll have a family meeting to share our findings. This isn't about pointing fingers but understanding our spending patterns and thinking of ways to improve. Perhaps we'll discover that those small snack purchases add up or find expenses we can cut down on. It's all about gaining insights into our personal spending habits and brainstorming ways to be smarter with our money.

Tips for success:

- Encourage honesty and openness. There's no shame in any spending habits. It's all about learning.
- Highlight positive spending behaviors and suggest ways to support each other in making better choices.

Investment Simulation

Ready to play the stock market without the risk? Let's set up a family investment challenge using fake money. We can use an online stock market simulator or create our own with play money and a list of companies we're interested in. Each family member gets a set amount to pretend invest in stocks they choose. Over a month, track the performance of those investments, learning about the stock market's ups and downs. This challenge demystifies investing and teaches us the value of research and patience when growing our money.

Tips for success:

- Use real-life companies that everyone is familiar with to spark interest.
- Schedule weekly "family board meetings" to discuss investment strategies and what we've learned about the stock market.

Budgeting Challenge

Who can make their money last the longest while still covering all their needs? This challenge is all about stretching our dollars and understanding the importance of budgeting. Each family member plans a budget with their allocated money for the week, including expenses such as snacks, entertainment, and savings. The goal is to meet all our needs without running out of money. It's a practical, hands-on way to learn about prioritizing spending and the satisfaction of making smart financial choices.

Tips for success:

- Provide a list of common expenses to help everyone plan their budget.
- Encourage creativity in finding ways to save money, like eating homemade snacks instead of store-bought.
- Share budgeting tips and tricks at the end of the challenge to help each other improve.

These challenges are stepping stones toward building strong financial habits that will serve us well into the future. Plus, embarking on these adventures as a family makes the journey more enjoyable and strengthens our bond as we work together toward common goals. So let's dive in and add a dash of fun to our financial learning.

9.3 CREATIVE SAVINGS PROJECTS: DIY PIGGY BANKS

Saving money turns into an adventure when you can see your progress. It's like playing a video game where every coin saved gets you closer to unlocking a new level or a coveted item. This thrill is what makes visual savings aids so powerful. They transform the abstract concept of saving into something tangible, something you can see and feel. And what better way to kickstart this visual savings journey than with a DIY project?

Making Saving Visual

Imagine your savings as a colorful progress bar in a game, filling up slowly as you move closer to your goal. This is the magic of visual savings aids. They give your goals shape and color, making the act of saving more immediate and rewarding. Each coin or bill saved becomes a visual reminder of your progress, keeping motivation high and the end goal in sight.

DIY Piggy Banks

Let's roll up our sleeves and create our own piggy banks. You don't need fancy materials. Most of what you need is probably lying around the house.

- **Balloon and papier-mâché piggy bank**: Start with a balloon as your base, and layer strips of newspaper soaked in a glue and water mixture to create papier-mâché. Once dry, pop the balloon, paint the newspaper, and there you have it —a custom-made piggy bank. Cut a slot for money, and maybe craft a cork or papier-mâché stopper for the bottom.
- **Recycled bottle bank**: Take a clean plastic bottle, cut a money slot, and let your creativity loose with paints, stickers, or glitter. It's a great way to reuse and recycle, turning waste into a treasure chest.
- **Shadow box savings frame**: Transform a shadow box frame into a piggy bank with a purpose. Decorate the background with your savings goal, such as a picture of a bicycle, a game console, or a travel destination. Cut a slot on top for money. As you add money, you can watch your savings cover the picture until it fully disappears, providing you a clear visual goal.

Customizing Savings Goals

Personalizing your piggy banks connects you more deeply with your savings goals. It's like naming your character in a game; it makes the journey more personal. Here are some ideas:

- **Goal stickers**: Use stickers or draw directly on your piggy bank to represent your savings goal. If it's a new bike, how about some bike stickers? If it's a trip, maybe some travel icons or destinations.
- **Color coding**: Assign different colors to different goals. If you're saving for a concert ticket, you could paint your piggy bank in the artist's album colors or use the concert theme.
- **Savings tracker**: Attach a small chart or tracker to your piggy bank where you can mark your progress. Moving a clip or filling in a bar as you save can be incredibly satisfying.

9.4 FINANCIAL LITERACY MOVIE NIGHT: LEARNING FROM FILMS

Grab some popcorn and dim the lights—it's time for a movie night with a twist! Movies have a way of sticking with us, their stories and characters lingering long after the credits roll. But did you know they can also teach us valuable lessons about handling money? From documentaries that unravel the mysteries of the stock market to animated adventures with hidden economic lessons, films can be a fun and effective way to boost your financial smarts.

Educational Films on Finance

Movies and documentaries are fantastic tools for understanding complex topics like economics and personal finance. Here are a few that families can enjoy together:

- *The Secret Millionaire's Club* (2009): An animated series where Warren Buffett mentors a group of kids in making wise financial decisions and starting their own business ventures. It's both educational and entertaining, covering basic principles of economics and entrepreneurship.

- *Money Smart for Young People*: A series of videos developed by the FDIC that offers lessons in financial literacy for various age groups, including young children. These videos cover topics like saving, budgeting, and the importance of making smart financial decisions.
- *Biz Kid$* (2008): This Emmy Award-winning educational show teaches kids about money management and entrepreneurship. Each episode covers a different financial topic through real-life stories of young entrepreneurs and practical advice from experts.
- *Finance 101*: Money Management for Kids (YouTube Series): Various YouTube channels offer series tailored to teaching kids about finance. These videos can range from explaining basic concepts of money, saving tips, understanding the value of money, and introductory lessons on investing.
- *The Tooth Fairy* (2010) (PG): While not strictly educational, this family comedy starring Dwayne "The Rock" Johnson can be used to introduce discussions about money with younger children, such as the concept of the tooth fairy and the value of a dollar.
- *The Boy Who Harnessed the Wind* (2019) (PG): This inspirational film shows how innovation and determination can lead to creating solutions that improve communities. It can be used to discuss the value of resources, investment in education, and sustainable development.
- *Once Upon a Dime* (1949): Though older, this animated short film by the Federal Reserve Bank of New York explains how money was invented, the importance of savings, and how banks lend money. It's a timeless piece that simplifies complex concepts.

- *WALL-E* (G): At first glance, it's a story about robots and love, but it's also a commentary on consumerism, sustainability, and corporate monopolies.
- *Inside Job* (PG-13): This documentary provides a detailed analysis of the factors leading to the 2008 financial crisis. Best suited for older kids, it's a thorough backgrounder on economic policies and practices.

Watching these films can open up a world of discussion about financial principles, ethics, and the impact of economic decisions on the wider world.

Creating a Movie Log

Keep the learning going by starting a movie log. This can be a simple notebook or a digital document where you list:

- The films you've watched together.
- Key financial concepts or lessons each film covered.
- Personal reflections on the film's message and how it applies to your financial situation or goals.

This log serves as a living document of your financial education journey through films. It's a place to reflect on what you've learned and how you've grown in your understanding of money matters. Plus, it can be a great resource to revisit as you encounter new financial decisions or challenges.

The magic of movies lies in their ability to teach, inspire, and entertain all at once. By incorporating films into your financial literacy efforts, you're not just learning about money, you're experiencing stories that bring those lessons to life in vivid, memorable ways. This approach to financial education proves that learning about money doesn't have to be dull or daunting. With a little creativity, it can be as engaging and enjoyable as a movie night with your favorite snacks and people.

As we wrap up our exploration of financial literacy through fun and games, remember the key takeaway: Learning about money management can and should be an enjoyable experience. Whether it's through board games, family challenges, creative projects, or movie nights, there are countless ways to engage with financial concepts outside of textbooks and classrooms. These activities teach valuable lessons and foster discussions, creativity, and bonding among family members. So keep the popcorn popping, the dice rolling, and the conversations flowing as you continue on your path to financial savvy. Now, let's turn the page and discover new adventures in the next chapter, ready to build on our understanding and dive deeper into the world of personal finance.

CHAPTER 10
THE ART OF NEGOTIATION: YOUR FINANCIAL SUPERPOWER

Picture yourself at a garage sale. You spot a vintage skateboard, the kind you've seen in movies but never up close. The price tag reads more than you have in your pocket, but you feel a tug in your heart. It has to be yours. Now, what if I told you that with a bit of talking and a sprinkle of charm, you might skate away with it for less than the sticker price? That's right, we're talking about negotiation, a skill as valuable as any coin in your piggy bank.

Negotiation isn't just for business moguls in suits. It's a daily part of life, from deciding who gets the last slice of pepperoni pizza to convincing your parents why you deserve a bigger allowance. When it comes to money, knowing how to negotiate can save you a few bucks and teach you important lessons about value, communication, and compromise.

Basic Negotiation Principles

The foundation of any good negotiation lies in understanding its core principles. At its heart, negotiation is a conversation aimed at reaching an agreement where both parties feel valued and satisfied. Here's the kicker: It's not about winning or getting a one-up on the other person. Instead, it's about finding common ground and crafting a deal that benefits everyone involved. Remember, the best deals are those where everyone walks away happy.

Role-Playing Scenarios

One of the best ways to sharpen your negotiation skills is through role-playing. Why not grab a friend or family member and practice? You could simulate buying a car, setting up a lemonade stand, or even negotiating which movie to watch on family night. Through role-playing, you:

- learn how to think on your feet.
- get comfortable with back-and-forth dialogue.
- discover the importance of listening and adjusting your strategy based on what the other person says.

Negotiation Tactics

Armed with an understanding of negotiation's core principles and some practice under your belt, it's time to dive into tactics that can help swing things in your favor:

- **Research is your best friend**: Always go into a negotiation well-informed. Knowing the value of what you're negotiating for can give you the upper hand.
- **Ask open-ended questions**: These require more than just a yes or no answer, encouraging the other person to share more information, which you can use to your advantage.
- **Be ready to walk away**: Sometimes, the best deal is the one you don't make. If it doesn't feel right, be prepared to walk

away. This shows you're not desperate, often bringing the other party back to the table with a better offer.

Ethical Considerations

In every negotiation, integrity matters. It's easy to get caught up in the moment, stretch the truth, or make promises you can't keep. Here's the thing: Honesty and transparency lead to fairer outcomes and build your reputation as someone who is trustworthy. So always negotiate with ethics at the forefront. Remember, a good deal today based on dishonesty can lead to lost opportunities tomorrow.

Interactive Element: Negotiation Practice Journal

As always, writing about your experiences helps you understand what happened and notice trends that were successful and those that weren't. Use a journal with prompts designed to reflect on your negotiation experiences. In each entry, detail:

- the scenario that led to the negotiations.
- the tactics you used and their effectiveness.
- lessons learned and areas for improvement.

This journal becomes a personal playbook, helping you refine your negotiation skills over time.

Negotiation is like a dance. It takes two to tango, and knowing the steps can make the difference between stepping on toes and gliding gracefully across the floor. Whether you're haggling at a yard sale, debating chores and allowances, or navigating the bigger financial decisions that life throws your way, negotiation is a superpower worth developing. It teaches you about value, respect, and the art of compromise. So the next time you find yourself eyeing that vintage skateboard or any other treasure, remember, a little negotiation can go a long way.

10.2 NEGOTIATING ALLOWANCES: A GUIDE FOR KIDS AND PARENTS

Negotiating an allowance is a dance between kids and parents, a way to understand each other's perspectives and reach a happy middle ground. Here's how to make sure both sides come out feeling good about the agreement.

Setting the Stage

Before even thinking about sitting down to discuss allowances, both parents and kids must do a bit of homework.

- **Parents**: Consider what chores are being done and whether you believe your child could handle additional responsibilities. Reflect on the purpose of the allowance: Is it for teaching money management, rewarding hard work, or both?
- **Kids**: Think about what you currently contribute to the household and whether there's more you could do. Also, understand why you want or need an increase. Is it to save for something specific, cover more of your personal expenses, or something else?

A clear understanding of these points sets a solid foundation for a productive conversation.

Presenting Your Case

When it's time to negotiate, presenting your case clearly and confidently makes all the difference.

- **Be prepared**: Come to the table with a list of your current chores, responsibilities, and ideas for additional tasks you're willing to take on.
- **Know your "why"**: Be ready to explain why you're asking for more money. Whether it's saving for a new bike or wanting to manage more of your own spending, your reasons should be clear and reasonable.
- **Stay calm and respectful**: Even if the conversation doesn't go your way immediately, keeping a level head shows maturity. Remember, this is a discussion, not a demand.

Reaching an Agreement

Finding common ground is the goal. Here's how to navigate toward a deal that feels fair to everyone.

- **Listen**: Both sides should be open to hearing each other out. Parents might have valuable insights on budgeting and saving, while kids can share their perspectives on the value of their work and financial needs.
- **Compromise**: Maybe the exact amount you were hoping for isn't feasible, but there could be room for compromise. Additional chores could lead to a bonus, or there might be other ways to earn through special projects.
- **Consider increments**: Rather than a big bump all at once, suggest gradual increases tied to taking on more responsibilities. This approach allows for growth and adjustment over time.

Written Agreements

Putting things in writing clarifies expectations and commitments from both sides.

- **Outline responsibilities and rewards**: Clearly state what chores are expected and what the allowance will be. Include any conditions, like quality of work or completion deadlines.
- **Include opportunities for review**: Set dates to revisit the agreement. This could be every few months or tied to school terms. It's a chance to discuss what's working, what isn't, and whether any adjustments are needed.
- **Sign it together**: Having both parent and child sign the agreement solidifies the commitment. It's a physical

reminder of the conversation and the promises made by both parties.

Negotiating an allowance is about more than just money. It's a learning experience that involves understanding value, articulating needs and wants, and working together to find solutions. For kids, it's a step toward financial literacy and independence, grounded in real-life practice of negotiation and compromise. For parents, it's an opportunity to guide and support your child's growth, encouraging responsibility and smart money management.

10.3 BARGAIN HUNTING: HOW TO GET THE BEST DEALS

Shopping smart doesn't just keep your wallet happy. It's like a game where the prize is getting more bang for your buck. Whether you're scouting the local yard sale for a hidden gem or navigating the vast ocean of online shopping, snagging a great deal feels like winning a treasure hunt. Let's unlock some secrets to becoming a savvy shopper, ensuring you always bag the best deals.

Researching Prices

Start your quest for the perfect bargain by doing a bit of detective work. Before you commit to buying anything, take a moment to look around. The internet has several comparison tools and websites that are user-friendly enough for kids and allow you to see how prices stack up across different stores. Be sure to ask a trusted adult for some help and watch out for scams. Below are some options known for their reliability and simplicity.

1. **Google Shopping**: Google Shopping is a straightforward tool that allows users to compare prices for products across different retailers. It's user-friendly and provides a broad range of products, making it a great starting point for kids under supervision.
2. **ShopSavvy**: ShopSavvy is an app that lets users scan barcodes or search for products to find the best prices online and in-store. Its simple interface can be navigated easily with a little guidance, making it suitable for older kids.
3. **Honey**: Honey is a browser extension that automatically finds and applies coupon codes at checkout but also offers a price comparison tool. While it's more about saving than comparing, it does provide price history charts and alerts for price drops, which can be educational for kids to learn about timing their purchases.
4. **CamelCamelCamel**: Specifically for Amazon products, CamelCamelCamel offers price history charts and price drop alerts. It's a web-based tool that's easy to use and can

help kids learn about price trends and the best times
to buy.

5. **PriceGrabber**: PriceGrabber provides a comprehensive
   platform for comparing prices across various products and
   retailers. It's detailed and offers extensive search filters that
   can help teach kids about making informed purchasing
   decisions.

While these tools can save you a lot of moolah, it's important to have
a parent or trusted adult supervise your use of these apps and
websites. Never make purchases without parental consent and always
protect your personal information online!

Timing Purchases

Timing is everything, and that couldn't be more true than when
you're shopping. Ever notice how swimsuits are a steal in winter or
how holiday decorations are practically given away in January? That's
because off-season shopping can lead to some serious savings.
Retailers need to clear out old stock to make room for new arrivals,
which means discounts for you. If you can wait a bit to buy that new
skateboard or winter coat, timing your purchase right can lead to big
savings.

- Buy off-season items for the next year.
- Keep an eye on holiday sales and end-of-season clearances.
- Ask your parent if you can subscribe to store newsletters to
  get a heads-up on upcoming sales.

Haggling Tips

Haggling may seem old-school, but it's an art that can still save you
some serious cash, especially at yard sales, flea markets, and even some

retail stores that are willing to match prices of other stores. The key is to be polite and reasonable. No one likes a pushy haggler. Start by expressing genuine interest in the item, then ask if the price is negotiable. Sometimes, just by asking, you'll get a better deal. And if you're buying multiple items, see if there's a discount for bundling them together. Remember, the worst they can say is no, but the best? You walk away with a great deal and a story to tell.

- Always be polite and respectful when haggling.
- Suggest a fair price that's lower than what you're willing to pay, giving you some room to meet in the middle.
- If the seller can't lower the price, see if they can throw in something extra to sweeten the deal.

10.4 CONFLICT RESOLUTION: MONEY AND FRIENDSHIPS

When money mixes with friendships, the blend can sometimes turn bittersweet. It's not uncommon for pals to find themselves in a pickle over unpaid loans or differing opinions on joint spending. But here's the good news: Navigating these choppy waters doesn't have to spell disaster for your relationships. With the right approach, resolving financial disagreements can actually strengthen bonds, proving that friendships can flourish even when money matters get complicated.

Money conflicts among friends often sprout from situations like one friend not paying back a loan on time or squabbling over splitting the cost of something you want to buy together. These moments, though small, can test the fabric of your friendship. Yet they also offer a chance for growth, teaching valuable lessons about empathy, understanding, and the importance of talking things through.

Speaking of talking it out, that is the golden key to resolving financial disagreements. Here's a simple truth: Most conflicts are born from misunderstandings, and a calm, honest chat can clear up confusion. When a money issue arises:

- Start the conversation with how you feel, using "I" statements to avoid placing blame. ("I feel confused because you said you would pay me, but you haven't.")
- Listen actively, giving your friend space to share their side of the story.
- Aim to understand their viewpoint, even if you don't entirely agree.

Think of solving problems with friends like playing a team sport. Fairness and compromise are the key players that make sure everyone wins. Sometimes, when you're trying to decide what to do together, not everyone will agree right away. You might want to go big—like buying the coolest, most expensive gift for a friend's birthday. But what if one of your teammates doesn't have enough allowance to pitch in?

Instead of sticking to the original plan and leaving someone out, you could come up with a new game plan. Maybe find a gift that's just as awesome but doesn't cost as much, or think of other ways your friend could help, like planning a surprise birthday game or making a homemade card. This way, everyone gets to contribute in their own way, and no one feels left out. The game is fun and fair for everyone —and that's how you score a true friendship win.

Setting clear expectations and boundaries around money from the get-go can steer friendships clear of potential pitfalls. Here are a few ideas:

- When lending money, agree on repayment terms beforehand. A simple "Can you pay me back by the end of the month?" can set a clear expectation.

- For shared expenses, use apps that track and split costs transparently. This way, everyone knows who owes what, leaving little room for confusion.
- Have open conversations about financial comfort zones. Understanding each other's limits can prevent awkward situations where someone feels pressured to overspend.

Money doesn't have to be a wedge that drives friends apart. When tackled with care, honesty, and a dash of creativity, financial disagreements can be resolved in ways that actually reinforce trust and understanding. And remember, the true value of a friendship isn't measured in dollars and cents but in the support, laughter, and memories shared along the way.

Navigating money matters with friends can certainly test the waters, but it doesn't have to capsize the ship. By fostering open communication, embracing fairness and compromise, and setting clear boundaries, these challenges can transform into opportunities for growth. Through this process, we learn about managing money and the invaluable skill of maintaining and strengthening our relationships. As we transition to the next chapter, we carry forward these lessons, ready to explore new dimensions of financial literacy and personal growth, always remembering the importance of empathy, respect, and understanding in every aspect of our lives.

CHAPTER 11
THE MONEY WIZARD'S PLAYBOOK

In a world where lemonade stands get upgraded to online stores and piggy banks turn digital, young minds are not just participating in the financial world, they're reshaping it. With fresh perspectives, they're solving old problems in new ways, proving that age is just a number when it comes to innovation. Let's take a closer look at how these young innovators are shaking things up and how you, too, might join this league of extraordinary thinkers.

Youth Financial Innovators

Imagine a teenager who's noticed how her friends struggle to save money. Instead of shrugging it off, she develops an app that rounds up their purchases to the nearest dollar, stashing the change away into a savings account. Or picture a group of kids who've started a recycling business, trading cans and bottles for cash and using the proceeds to fund community projects. These aren't just hypothetical scenarios. They're real stories of kids and teens identifying gaps and opportunities in their world and stepping in with solutions.

- Savings apps developed by teens for their peers focus on user-friendly design and gamification to make saving fun.
- Youth-led environmental businesses turn ecological action into economic opportunity by recycling or crafting eco-friendly products.

Their success lies not just in their ideas but in their approach. They see a need, imagine a way to fill it, and dare to try.

Encouraging Innovation

You might wonder, "How can I start thinking like an innovator?" Here are a few strategies:

- **Stay curious**: Ask questions about how things work and why. Often, innovation starts with a simple, "What if... ?"

- **Observe and listen**: Pay attention to conversations around you, especially complaints or wishes for "something better." These can be golden opportunities for innovation.
- **Learn by doing**: Don't be afraid to experiment. Whether it's coding a simple app or starting a small project, hands-on experience is invaluable.

Remember, every big breakthrough begins with a small step. The key is to start.

The Role of Mentorship

Behind many young innovators is a mentor, someone who's been there, done that, and is willing to guide you through the process of turning ideas into reality. Finding a mentor can:

- **Boost your confidence**: Sometimes, just knowing someone believes in you can push you to keep going.
- **Provide practical advice**: From technical skills to navigating challenges, mentors can offer insights you might not find anywhere else.
- **Expand your network**: Mentors often introduce you to others who can help, opening doors you didn't even know existed.

So, how do you find a mentor? Start by reaching out to teachers, family friends, or professionals in fields you're interested in. Be clear about what you hope to achieve with your mentor and why you think they'd be the right fit.

Future of Money: Predictions From Young Minds

In a world where piggy banks are becoming more virtual than actual and allowance transactions can happen with a quick tap on a screen, it's clear that the concept of money is evolving right before our eyes. Now imagine if we handed the crystal ball to the younger generation, the true digital natives. What kind of future financial landscape do they foresee?

Kids' Predictions

When we listen to kids' predictions about the future of money, their ideas range from wildly imaginative to eerily plausible. Some envision a world where cryptocurrencies are as common as cash once was, used to buy everything from a spaceship ride to candy at the corner store. Others foresee a shift toward a more barter-based system, leveraging technology to trade skills instead of currency. Imagine an app that lets you exchange piano lessons for coding classes. The common thread in these predictions is a move toward more personalized and direct exchanges of value facilitated by technology.

- Cryptocurrencies as common currency
- A resurgence of barter systems, enhanced by tech platforms

Learning From the Past

To truly appreciate these forward-looking visions, it's helpful to glance back at how money has changed over the centuries. From trading shells and salt to the introduction of paper money and then to plastic cards, each evolution was sparked by the need for more convenience and security. These historical shifts show us that while the form of money may change, its core purpose—to facilitate exchange—remains constant. This historical lens helps kids understand that their predictions aren't just fanciful dreams but part of an ongoing evolution.

The Impact of Technology

Technology's role in shaping our financial systems cannot be overstated. Kids today are growing up in an era where digital wallets are more common than physical ones. They see the potential for tech not just to change how we spend or save but to make financial systems more inclusive and accessible. For instance, imagine a world where blockchain technology ensures every child has access to a savings account from birth or where AI advisors help people make smarter spending decisions, leveling the playing field for financial literacy.

- Digital wallets becoming the norm
- Blockchain and AI as tools for financial inclusivity and literacy

Creative Envisioning

To harness these imaginative ideas, schools and communities are increasingly holding workshops and contests that challenge kids to design their versions of the future of finance. Kids articulate their visions through drawing, writing, or even building models, from money that grows on trees to accounts that automatically donate a percentage to charity. These activities spark creativity and give kids a sense of ownership over their future, encouraging them to think critically about the role of money in society and their lives.

- Workshops and contests for kids to design the future of finance
- Fostering a sense of ownership and critical thinking about money

As we wrap up this exploration into the future of money through the eyes of our youngest visionaries, it's clear that their ideas hold the seeds of possibility. They envision a world where money is not just a means of transaction but a tool for empowerment, creativity, and global connection. By listening to their predictions and understanding the historical journey of money, we're reminded that the essence of finance is always evolving, shaped by our collective needs, dreams, and innovations. As we turn the page, let's carry forward this sense of possibility and openness to change, ready to embrace whatever the future holds.

CONCLUSION

Well, folks, we've officially reached the treasure chest at the end of our grand financial literacy adventure. From the humble beginnings of understanding the almighty dollar (or whatever currency floats your boat) to the lofty ideals of saving, spending wisely, and investing like mini moguls. We've navigated the tricky waters of credit, dived into the digital dollars of the future, and even learned how to turn hobbies into cold, hard cash (or at least a steady trickle of digital currency).

Starting young on this journey gives you a head start and sets up a solid foundation for your financial house (which you're now more equipped to save for). The habits you've started forming, the knowledge you've soaked up like a sponge, and the attitude you've developed toward money are more precious than the contents of any piggy bank. They're the keys to a kingdom where your financial well-being reigns supreme.

Let's review the golden nuggets we've unearthed together:

- Save like a squirrel stashing nuts for the winter.
- Spend with the wisdom of a sage, not like a kid in a candy store.
- Invest with the curiosity of a cat but the caution of a turtle.
- Understand credit as if your superhero cape depended on it.
- Embrace the global economy like you're giving the world a giant bear hug.

And, in the spirit of breaking the mold, remember that creativity and innovation in managing your moolah can lead to some epic financial wins. Don't be afraid to unleash your inner financial wizard, leverage tech to make your money work smarter, not harder, and explore the entrepreneurial wilderness with gusto.

This is hardly the end, my young apprentices. It's merely the beginning of a lifelong quest for financial savvy. The world of finance is as vast and changing as the ocean, with new concepts to explore, technologies to harness, and strategies to master. Keep that curiosity alive, and never stop seeking knowledge and adventure in personal finance.

Now, I challenge you to take action. Start small, dream big, and celebrate every victory along the way. Whether it's setting up your first budget, opening a savings account, or investing in your first stock, every step forward is a step toward your financial independence.

Don't keep all this newfound wisdom to yourself. Share the wealth (of knowledge) with your family, friends, and even your loyal pet (hey, they might enjoy the sound of your voice). Teaching and discussing these topics reinforces your learning and can inspire those around you to start their own financial literacy journey.

I'm tipping my hat to you for embarking on this adventure. Your dedication to navigating the sometimes choppy, sometimes exhilarating waters of personal finance is nothing short of heroic. As you sail into the future, remember that your potential to make wise decisions and achieve financial success is as boundless as the sea. Envision a future where you are the captain of your financial destiny, steering toward your dreams with confidence and skill.

Here's to you, future financial champions. May your wallets be heavy, your hearts light, and your journey rich with learning and growth. Onward and upward!

PASSING THE TORCH OF FINANCIAL WISDOM

Congratulations, young savers and spenders! You've navigated through the twists and turns of The Ultimate Guide to Financial Literacy for Kids and emerged with a treasure trove of knowledge about money, saving, and investing. You're now equipped with the tools to carve out a path to financial success and security.

But as you stand at this exciting crossroads, with the power to make smart financial choices in your hands, there's one more quest that lies ahead. It's time to share the wealth of knowledge you've gained and light the way for others on their financial journey.

By leaving your honest review of this book on Amazon, you're not just sharing your thoughts but guiding future financial adventurers to the map that helped you discover the secrets of money management. Your review is a beacon, illuminating the path for others seeking guidance and inspiration to embark on their own quest for financial literacy.

Your voice matters, and your experience could be the key to unlocking a world of opportunity for someone else. By passing on your passion for financial literacy, you're contributing to a brighter future for all.

Thank you for being an integral part of keeping the spirit of financial education alive. Together, we're not just learning about money; we're building a community of informed, responsible, and empowered individuals.

Scan the QR code to share your journey and leave your review on Amazon.

https://www.amazon.com/review/create-review/?asin=
B0CZDGZGFG

Your insight and enthusiasm are the sparks that can ignite a passion for financial literacy in others. By sharing your review, you're ensuring that the flame of knowledge burns brightly for generations to come.

Thank you for joining us on this adventure and helping spread the magic of financial literacy. Your contribution is invaluable; together, we're making a difference, one review at a time.

With gratitude, Your friends at Money Mentor Publications

BIBLIOGRAPHY

1. Bankrate. (n.d.). Investing basics for kids: How to teach children to save and invest. Retrieved from https://www.bankrate.com/investing/how-to-teach-kids-about-investing/

2. Big Life Journal. (n.d.). 7 Fun Goal-Setting Activities for Children. Retrieved from https://biglifejournal.com/blogs/blog/5-fun-goal-setting-activities-children

3. Britannica Kids. (n.d.). Sustainability - Kids | Britannica Kids | Homework Help. Retrieved from https://kids.britannica.com/kids/article/sustainability/631786

4. Business Insider. (2024, February). Best Investment Apps for Beginners in February 2024. Retrieved from https://www.businessinsider.com/personal-finance/best-investment-apps-for-beginners

5. Campbellsville University Online. (n.d.). Benefits of Financial Literacy for Kids. Retrieved from https://online.campbellsville.edu/education/financial-literacy-for-kids/

6. Carosa, C. (2021, May 22). True Stories Of Children Saving Successfully. Forbes. Retrieved from https://www.forbes.com/sites/chriscarosa/2021/05/22/true-stories-of-children-saving-successfully/

7. Clear, J. (n.d.). The Marshmallow Experiment and the Power of Delayed Gratification. Retrieved from https://jamesclear.com/delayed-gratification

8. CNN Money. (2015, April 28). Meet the 17-year-old investor who tripled his money. Retrieved from https://money.cnn.com/2015/04/28/investing/millennial-investor-17-year-old-brandon-fleisher/

9. Cool Crafts. (n.d.). 40 Cool DIY Piggy Banks For Kids & Adults. Retrieved from https://www.coolcrafts.com/cool-diy-piggy-banks/

10. Credit Canada. (n.d.). How Financial Technology is Changing the Way Kids Learn About Money. Retrieved from https://www.creditcanada.com/blog/how-financial-technology-is-changing-the-way-kids-learn-about-money

11. DebtConsolidationUSA. (n.d.). 6 Movies With Great Money Lessons For Kids. Retrieved from https://www.debtconsolidationusa.com/personal-finance/6-movies-great-money-lessons-kids.html

12. Ducksters. (n.d.). Money and Finance: History of Money. Retrieved from https://www.ducksters.com/money/history_of_money.php

13. ElementaryEdu. (2022, July). How to Teach The Difference Between Wants and Needs (11 Strategies). Retrieved from https://elementaryedu.com/2022/07/the-difference-between-wants-and-needs.html

14. Freedomsprout. (n.d.). 53 Board Games to Teach Your Kids About Money (At Every Age). Retrieved from https://freedomsprout.com/money-board-games/

15. GoHenry. (n.d.). 18 Fun Money Activities for Kids. Retrieved from https://www.gohenry.com/us/blog/financial-education/18-fun-money-activities-for-kids

16. GoHenry. (n.d.). Should you get a prepaid card for your kids? (pros + cons). Retrieved from https://www.gohenry.com/us/blog/financial-education/should-you-get-a-prepaid-card-for-your-kids

17. GoHenry. (n.d.). Teaching kids about credit in simple terms. Retrieved from https://www.gohenry.com/us/blog/financial-education/teaching-kids-about-credit-in-simple-terms

18. GoHenry. (n.d.). The 8 best budgeting & money apps for kids & teens. Retrieved from https://www.gohenry.com/uk/blog/financial-education/the-best-budgeting-apps-for-families

19. GoHenry. (n.d.). Teaching Your Child To Recognize and Avoid Internet Scams. Retrieved from https://www.gohenry.com/us/blog/online-safety/teaching-your-child-to-recognize-and-avoid-internet-scams

20. Good Housekeeping. (2002, November). Money Lessons for Kids. Retrieved from https://www.goodhousekeeping.com/life/money/advice/a12132/money-lessons-kids-nov02/

21. Investopedia. (n.d.). 10 Successful Young Entrepreneurs. Retrieved from https://www.investopedia.com/10-successful-young-entrepreneurs-4773310

22. Investopedia. (n.d.). How to Teach Your Child About Cryptocurrency. Retrieved from https://www.investopedia.com/how-to-teach-your-child-about-cryptocurrency-5224013

23. Investopedia. (n.d.). How to Teach Your Child About Investing. Retrieved from https://www.investopedia.com/articles/pf/07/childinvestor.asp

24. Kiplinger. (n.d.). My 10 Best Financial Literacy Apps for Kids. Retrieved from https://www.kiplinger.com/article/saving/t065-c032-s014-my-10-best-financial-literacy-apps-for-kids.html

25. LinkedIn. (n.d.). Negotiation Training Games: Fun and Effective Ways to Improve Your Skills. Retrieved from https://www.linkedin.com/pulse/negotiation-training-games-fun-effective-ways-improve

26. Money Geek. (n.d.). Money Foundations for Kids: Compound Interest. Retrieved from https://www.moneygeek.com/financial-planning/compound-interest-for-kids/

27. MoneySupermarket.com. (n.d.). How to teach kids to be ethical consumers as adults. Retrieved from https://www.moneysupermarket.com/news/how-to-teach-kids-to-be-ethical-consumers-as-adults

28. MyDoh. (n.d.). How to Help Kids and Teens Avoid Impulse Buying. Retrieved from https://www.mydoh.ca/learn/blog/lifestyle/how-to-help-kids-and-teens-avoid-impulse-buying/

29. MyDoh. (n.d.). How to Teach Your Kids Negotiation Skills. Retrieved from https://www.mydoh.ca/learn/blog/lifestyle/how-to-teach-your-kids-negotiation-skills/

30. MyDoh. (n.d.). 10 Money Mistakes Teens Make and How to Avoid Them. Retrieved from https://www.mydoh.ca/learn/blog/banking/10-money-mistakes-teens-make-and-how-to-avoid-them/

31. Partner Colorado Credit Union. (n.d.). How to Start a Financial Journal. Retrieved from https://www.partnercoloradocu.org/resources/financial-education/savings/how-to-start-a-financial-journal

32. Pon Harvard Edu. (n.d.). Ethics and Negotiation: 5 Principles of Negotiation to Boost Your Bargaining Skills in Your Personal and Professional Life. Retrieved from https://www.pon.harvard.edu/daily/negotiation-training-daily/questions-of-ethics-in-negotiation/

33. QinPrinting. (n.d.). How to Design an Educational Board Game. Retrieved from https://www.qinprinting.com/blog/how-to-design-an-educational-board-game/

34. Quicken. (n.d.). 12 Fun Summer Money Challenges for Kids. Retrieved from https://www.quicken.com/blog/challenges-for-kids/

35. Ramsey Solutions. (n.d.). 15 Ways to Teach Kids About Money. Retrieved from https://www.ramseysolutions.com/relationships/how-to-teach-kids-about-money

36. Savvy Sparrow. (n.d.). 75 Rewards for Kids (and How to Make Rewards Work). Retrieved from https://thesavvysparrow.com/rewards-for-kids/

37. The Balance Money. (n.d.). Budgeting for Kids: How To Teach It and Why It Matters. Retrieved from https://www.thebalancemoney.com/teach-kids-to-budget-money-454012

38. Ameriprise Financial. (n.d.). Financial literacy for kids: Teaching kids about money. Retrieved from https://www.ameriprise.com/financial-goals-priorities/family-estate/6-simple-ways-to-raise-financially-savvy-kids

39. Bankaroo. (n.d.). 8 Tips for Keeping Your Kids Safe When Banking or Shopping Online. Retrieved from https://bankaroo.com/8-tips-for-keeping-your-kids-safe-when-banking-or-shopping-online/

40. Forbes Advisor. (n.d.). How To Open A Savings Account For A Child. Retrieved from https://www.forbes.com/advisor/banking/savings/guide-to-childrens-and-kids-savings-accounts/

41. ClassTechTips. (2023, May 03). How to Teach Sustainable Investing to Kids. Retrieved from https://classtechtips.com/2023/05/03/what-is-sustainable-investing/

ANSWER KEY

Chapter 1

Chapter 2

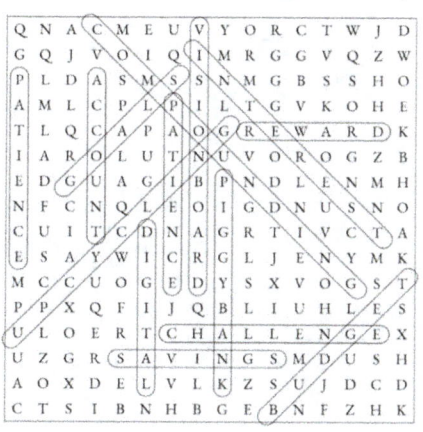

Chapter 3

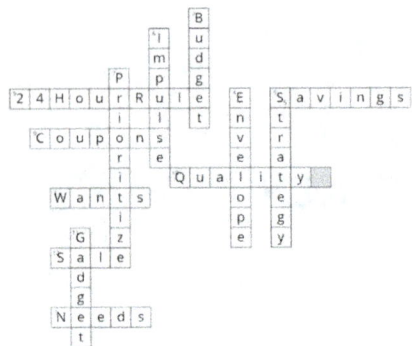

Chapter 6

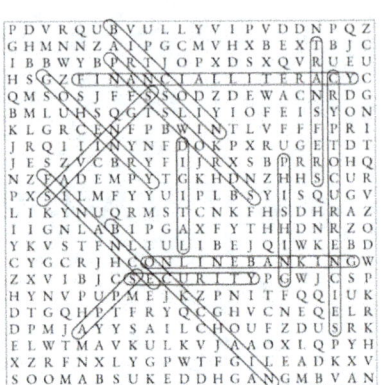

www.ingramcontent.com/pod-product-compliance
Lightning Source LLC
Chambersburg PA
CBHW071150120626
46546CB00006B/2193